FAST TRACK TO A 5

Preparing for the **AP**®
**Computer Science
Principles Examination**

Kathleen McLead
Strath Haven High School, Wallingford, PA

Tony Graham
Flour Bluff High School, Corpus Christi, TX

CENGAGE
Learning·

Australia • Brazil • Mexico • Singapore • United Kingdom • United States

ISBN: 978-1-337-28882-8

Cengage Learning
20 Channel Center Street
Boston, MA 02210
USA

Cengage Learning is a leading provider of customized learning solutions with office locations around the globe, including Singapore, the United Kingdom, Australia, Mexico, Brazil, and Japan. Locate your local office at: **www.cengage.com/global**.

Cengage Learning products are represented in Canada by Nelson Education, Ltd.

To learn more about Cengage Learning Solutions, visit **www.cengage.com**.

To find online supplements and other instructional support, please visit **www.cengagebrain.com**.

AP® is a trademark registered and/or owned by the College Board, which was not involved in the production of, and does not endorse, this product.

Printed in the United States of America
Print Number: 05   Print Year: 2017

CONTENTS

ABOUT THE AUTHORS

KATHLEEN M. MCLEAD, M.Ed. Secondary Education, Mathematics, has 16 years of experience, 11 teaching math and 5 teaching computer science. She spent three years participating in the AP® Computer Science Principles Pilot II program as a pilot instructor. She has been a presenter at CSTA>>Philly meetings and REThink CS@Drexel, highlighting her experiences in the CS Principles classroom and sharing the Processing programming language. Kathleen is passionate about exposing all students to computer science. The courses she teaches include AP® Computer Science A, AP® Computer Science Principles, Intro to Computer Science, Coding for Web Design, Video Game Design, and Advanced Video Game Design. Outside of her job as a computer science teacher at Strath Haven High School in Wallingford, Pennsylvania, Kathleen loves spending time with her husband Jason, also a teacher, and her two children, Mary and Henry. Computer Science and coding are frequent topics of conversation in the McLead house.

TONY GRAHAM, M.A. Computer Science, teaches AP® Computer Science Principles, AP® CSA, and various robotics courses at Flour Bluff High School in Corpus Christi, Texas. He has participated in computer science pilot courses for both the College Board and Project Lead the Way (PLTW). In addition to teaching computer science courses, Tony is also PLTW certified to teach multiple engineering courses. In the summer, he serves as a PLTW Master Teacher where he instructs middle and high school teachers from around the country how to implement the PLTW curriculum into their AP® CS Principles courses. Tony sponsors multiple FIRST FTC Robotics teams and has advanced teams to the FTC South Super Regionals. In the remainder of his spare time, Tony coaches youth soccer and youth baseball.

Part I

Preparing for the AP® Computer Science Principles Exam

PREPARING FOR THE AP® EXAM

Advanced Placement® Computer Science Principles can be creative, engaging, and rewarding. Whether you are taking an AP® course at your school or working independently, the stage is set for a great intellectual experience. As the school year progresses and you delve deeper and deeper into the course work, you will begin to make connections between the ideas and concepts that form the basis of computer science principles. Understanding these concepts with growing sophistication is exciting, but more exciting still is applying creative processes in developing computational thinking skills and creating computational artifacts while exploring questions and projects that are of interest to you. In an added dimension, the AP® Computer Science Principles course shows how computing has changed our world by focusing on the global impact that advances in computing have had and are currently having on people and society.

Sometime during the spring, as May approaches, the AP® exam will start to feel more like a tangible obstacle you will soon face. At times, the amount of material you must master to be successful on the Advanced Placement® exam may seem somewhat overwhelming or intimidating. If you are dreading the exam, just know that you are not the only one. However, there are some simple exam tips and review steps you can follow that will get you on the fast track to making that 5.

First and foremost, it is imperative to maintain the motivation and a positive attitude to guide your preparation. If you manage your time effectively, you will meet this one major challenge—mastery of a large amount of material in a short period of time. You should develop a review schedule to help direct your study time so that you spread out your review over the course of at least several weeks to a month prior to the exam rather than relying on just a few short days of cramming. This book is designed to put you on a fast track to success on the AP® Computer Science Principles exam. Sticking to your review schedule and allowing enough practice time prior to the exam will help you master the course material and will also give you an invaluable amount of confidence on the day of the exam.

WHAT'S IN THIS BOOK

Because this book follows the College Board Concept Outline for the course, it is compatible with all textbooks or online resources that you may be using in your class. It is divided into three sections. Part I offers

---

AP® is a trademarks registered and/or owned by the College Board, which was not involved in the production of, and does not endorse, this product.

suggestions for getting yourself ready, from signing up to take the test to understanding how you will be assessed on the combined through-course performance tasks and the end-of-course AP® exam.

Part II, made up of 7 chapters, present the 7 Big Ideas that constitute the foundation for the Computer Science Principles course. They are:

Big Idea 1: Creativity
Big Idea 2: Abstraction
Big Idea 3: Data and Information
Big Idea 4: Algorithms
Big Idea 5: Programming
Big Idea 6: The Internet
Big Idea 7: Global Impact

Each chapter provides a description of the Big Idea it covers and a table of all Learning Objectives and Essential Knowledge statements which are the assessment targets for the through-course performance tasks and the AP® exam. Chapters 2–7 also include a set of multiple-choice review questions to help you study and prepare for the end-of-course exam and an Answer Key that explains correct answers and provides Learning Objective and Essential Knowledge correlations for each question.

Part III has two complete AP® Computer Science Principles exams. At the end of each test, you will again find the answers, explanations, and Learning Objective references. The two test forms allow flexibility if you choose to use one as a Diagnostic Test early in your review, or if you want to save both forms for simulated exam practice after you have worked through the complete Fast Track book.

SETTING UP A REVIEW SCHEDULE

If you have been steadily doing your homework and keeping up with the course work, you are in good shape. But if you are still not sure you have mastered the AP material, or if you fell behind, there are some more ways to ensure that you are prepared for the test in time.

To begin, read Part I of this book. You will be much more comfortable going into the test if you understand how the test questions are designed and how best to approach them.

Take out a calendar and set up a schedule for yourself. If you begin studying early, you can comfortably work your way through the review chapters in Part II. You'll be surprised—and pleased—by how much material you can cover by studying a half an hour a day for a month or so before the test. Look carefully at the Learning Objectives and Essential Knowledge statements—these specify the facts and content you will be expected to know on the exam. If you missed a number of questions in one particular area, allow more time for reviewing your course materials related to that Big Idea. The practice tests in Part III will give you more experience with managing the full range of content in a timed simulated exam experience.

BEFORE THE EXAM

By February, long before the exam, you need to make sure that you are registered to take the test. Many schools take care of the paperwork and handle the fees for their AP® students, but check with your teacher or the AP® coordinator to make sure that you are on the list. This is especially important if you have a documented disability and need special arrangements for the test. If paying for the test presents a financial hardship for your family, don't be shy. Contact your school's AP® coordinator. The College Entrance Examination Board offers reduced fees for those who qualify. If you are studying independently, call AP® Services at the College Entrance Examination Board for the name of the local AP® coordinator, who will help you through the registration process.

The evening before the exam is not a great time for partying, nor is it a great time for cramming. If you like, look over class notes or drift through your course materials, concentrating on the broad outlines, not the small details. You may also want to skim through this book again.

The evening before the exam is a great time to get your things ready for the next day. Sharpen a fistful of No. 2 pencils with good erasers, and make sure you have your Social Security number and whatever photo identification and admission ticket are required. Make sure you have removed your cell phone from your backpack or purse. Cell phones are not allowed during the exam; if you want you can wear a watch to keep track of your time.

On the day of the examination, make sure you do not skip meals; studies show that students who eat a reasonable meal before testing tend to get higher grades. Be careful not to drink a lot of liquids, as this could make a trip to the restroom necessary during the test and cost you valuable time in the process. You will spend some time waiting while everyone is seated in the right room for the right test. That's before the test has even begun. The AP® Computer Science Principles Exam will then last for 2 hours. So be prepared to stay focused for that time. You do not want to be distracted by a growling stomach or hunger pangs.

Be sure to wear comfortable clothes, taking along a sweater in case the heating or air-conditioning is erratic. Be sure, too, to wear clothes you like—people always perform better when they feel that they look better—and by all means wear your lucky socks.

Now go out there and earn a 5!

TAKING THE AP® COMPUTER SCIENCE PRINCIPLES EXAM

The AP® Computer Science Principles course introduces you to seven Big Ideas: Computing is a creative activity; Abstraction reduces information and detail to facilitate focus on relative concepts; Data and information facilitate the creation of knowledge; Algorithms are used to develop and express solutions to computational problems; Programming enables problem solving, human expression, and creation of knowledge. The Internet pervades modern computing, and Computing has global impact. Throughout the course, while preparing for the final assessment as well as the through-course assessment, you will be expected to develop six Computational Thinking Practices: Connecting Computing, Creating computational artifacts, Abstracting, Analyzing problems and artifacts, Communicating, and Collaborating. These practices will help you become a strong digital citizen.

ASSESSMENT OVERVIEW

Your performance assessment in AP® Computer Science Principles consists of two components: two through-course performance tasks, worth 40% of the AP® Grade, and a Multiple Choice Exam, worth 60% of the AP® Grade. The Performance Tasks are given in class, but students are allowed to spend time on them outside of class. The first Performance Task, Explore – Impact of Computing Innovations, is worth 16% of the final AP® score. Students are given 8 hours of class time to investigate a computational innovation and create an artifact demonstrating its impact on society. The second Performance Task, Create – Applications from Ideas, is worth 24% of the final AP® score. Students are given 12 hours to create and describe a working program. These tasks are due April 30 of each year, though the College Board recommends completing them by April 15.

You can find much more information about preparing for and completing the through-course assessment performance tasks if you go to AP® Central online. The College Board has created a set of handouts for students that appear as pages 102-113 of the AP® Computer Science Principles Course and Exam Description. The handouts include useful information about preparing for the Explore and Create performance tasks, along with detailed requirements on completing and submitting your work. Your teacher may have already given you a set of these handouts, but you can also get them on your own by following this link:

https://secure-media.collegeboard.org/digitalServices/pdf/ap/ap-computer-science-principles-course-and-exam-description.pdf

---

AP® is a trademarks registered and/or owned by the College Board, which was not involved in the production of, and does not endorse, this product.

THE EXAM

The AP® Computer Science Principles Exam (60% of the AP® Score) consists of 74 multiple choice questions. You will have 120 minutes for the exam. There are two types of multiple choice questions: single-select and multiple-select. All multiple-select questions will be identified, and there will be exactly two correct answers. All questions have four answer choices. You will be tested on six of the seven Big Ideas (Big Idea 1: Creativity is assessed through the Performance Tasks).

The AP® Exam does not test any one particular programming language, so a Reference Sheet is provided for you to use throughout the course to help you prepare for what programming questions may look like. That Reference Sheet is also included here in Fast Track as an Appendix at the back of the book.

STRATEGIES FOR THE MULTIPLE-CHOICE QUESTIONS

Here are some rules of thumb to help you work your way through the multiple-choice questions:

NO GUESSING PENALTY There are four possible answers for each question. Each correct answer is awarded one point and no points are deducted for incorrect answers. Test takers should therefore not leave any answers blank.

READ THE QUESTION CAREFULLY Find questions you are confident of and work those first. (Generally the easier questions appear first on the exam.) Then return to the questions you skipped. Make a mark in the booklet on questions you are unsure of so that you can return to those questions later.

READ EACH QUESTION CAREFULLY Pressured for time, many students make the mistake of reading the questions too quickly or merely skimming them. By reading a question carefully, you may already have some idea about the correct answer. You can then look for it in the responses. Careful reading is especially important in EXCEPT questions and in questions with Roman numeral choices.

ELIMINATE ANY ANSWER YOU KNOW IS WRONG You may write on the multiple-choice questions in the test book. As you read through the answer choices, draw a line through any answer you know is wrong.

READ ALL OF THE POSSIBLE ANSWERS, THEN CHOOSE THE BEST ANSWER CHOICE AP® Exams are written to test your precise knowledge of a subject. Sometimes there are a few probable answers, but one of them is more specific or, when weighing the choices, a better response. For example, numbers can be expressed in several bases, but often certain bases are more appropriate than others in certain circumstances. For example, hexadecimal is most appropriate in referencing a memory location.

MARK AND SKIP TOUGH QUESTIONS If you are hung up on a question, mark it in the margin of the question book. Questions involving base conversion or programming, especially when there are loops involved, can be particularly time consuming. If you notice that it is a lengthy question or you do not immediately know the answer, then skip the question. You can come back to skipped questions later if you have time. Make sure you skip these questions on your answer sheet, too. You do not want to miss the opportunity to answer questions that you possibly know because you spend too much time on a particularly difficult question. Be sure to come back to these problems and give them your best, even if it is a guess, since there is no penalty for guessing.

TYPES OF MULTIPLE-CHOICE QUESTIONS

There are various kinds of multiple-choice questions. Here are some suggestions for how to approach each kind.

CLASSIC/BEST-ANSWER QUESTIONS

This is the most common type of multiple-choice question. It simply requires you to select the most correct answer. For example:

1. A set of operations on a list, such as "INSERT" or "FOR EACH item IN List" can be performed on the list regardless of the data type. Why?
    (A) Lists can contain a pre-established group of data types, with which all methods will work.
    (B) Lists can be treated as abstract data types in developing programs.
    (C) Lists inherit operations from collections.
    (D) Lists are immutable, meaning that the values stored in them never change.

    ANSWER: B. Choice B is Essential Knowledge statement EK 5.5.1I, which states "Lists and other collections can be treated as abstract data types (ADTs) in developing programs."

NOT QUESTIONS

A good way of tracking your assessment of each answer choice in a NOT-style question is to mark each true statement with a T and then identify the one false statement that you would mark with an F. The response option marked with an F is the one that does NOT fit the conditions of the question, and is therefore the correct answer.

2. While the technology of self-driving cars is in development now on a limited scale, it may be some time before driverless cars are seen widely on our roads. There are, however, several aspects of intelligent transportation that are in use today and can be very effective. Which of the choices below is NOT an example of a smart transportation system feature?
    (A) A crash avoidance system that vibrates a driver's seat when they are too close to a car beside or in front of them.
    (B) Sensors placed in the roads calculate the amount of traffic that is currently traveling and automatically adjusts the speed limit to maximize traffic efficiency.

(C) Controls placed on the steering wheel that allow the driver to control the radio, cruise control, and other internal systems of the vehicle.

(D) Traffic cameras that are placed at various intervals along a well-traveled road in order to enforce speed limits and send tickets to drivers who exceed the posted limits.

ANSWER: C. While controls such as these might be considered "smart", a primary component of intelligent transportation is that it takes place outside of the vehicle. You should have written as "F" next to this answer. All of the other options have some form of interaction from the outside on the vehicle (road sensors and traffic cameras) or from inside the vehicle to the outside (crash avoidance). They should all have "T"s written next to them.

LIST AND GROUP QUESTIONS

In this type of question, there is a list of possible answers, and you must select the answer that contains the correct group of responses. These questions look hard, but you can simplify them by crossing out items from the list and then eliminating them in the answers below. For example:

3. Consider the task of simulating the results of selecting a random row and a random column to represent a random location on a 10x10 grid. Which of the following code segments will assign the appropriate results for the location on the grid, as defined by a row number between 1 and 10 and a column number between 1 and 10?

```
I.   row ← RANDOM(1,10)
     column ← RANDOM(1,10)
II.  gridLocation ← (RANDOM(1,10) * RANDOM(1,10))
III. gridLocation ← (RANDOM(1,100))
     row ← gridLocation MOD 10
     column ← (gridLocation – row) / 10
```

(A) I only
(B) I and II only
(C) I and III only
(D) II and III only

ANSWER: A. Algorithm I selects two random numbers between 1 and 10, inclusive. To approach this question, begin by testing Algorithm I. The first line of code assigns a random value between 1 and 10 for a row, and the second line of code does the same for a column. Algorithm I works, so you should cross out any answer choices that don't include I. Draw a line through choice (D), since it does not include Algorithm I. Continue testing the Algorithms. Algorithm II multiplies two random values between 1 and 10, so all we get is a value between 1 and 100. Although this number could be a location on a grid, the problem specifically states that the location is represented by a row number and a column number. Draw lines through Algorithm II and choice (B). Algorithm III selects a random number between 1 and 100 and assigns it to gridLocation. It attempts to assign the row value to gridLocation MOD 10. This expression will never yield a 10 and could yield a 0, so you can draw a line through Algorithm III and choice (C). The only remaining answer choice is (A).

Multiple-Select Questions

Similar to the NOT questions, MULTIPLE-SELECT questions can be answered using the "T" or "F" method. Simply read the question, then write a "T" next to true statements and an "F" next to false statements. There will be two true and two false statements. Usually, you will select the two true statements, unless the question is also a NOT question.

4. Which of the following code segments executes three instructions if the initial condition is correct? Select <u>two</u> answers.

(A)
```
IF (x > 3)
{
   x ← x - 4
}
IF (x > 0)
{
   x ← x - 4
}
x ← 2 * x
```

(B)
```
IF (x > 3)
{
   x ← x + 4
}
IF (x > 0)
{
   x ← x - 4
}
x ← 2 * x
```

(C)
```
IF (x > 3)
{
   x ← x - 4
}
x ← 2 * x

IF (x > 0)
{
   x ← x - 4
}
```

(D)
```
IF (x > 3)
{
   x ← x + 4
}
x ← 2 * x

IF (x > 0)
{
   x ← x - 4
}
```

ANSWERS: B, D. In both code segments x will meet the requirements of the second "if" statement as long as the requirements of the first were met.

Assuming that $x > 3$, Choice A has you subtract 4 from x. You do not know if our new value for x will be greater than 0, so you should mark (A) with an "F". Choice B has you add 4 to x, so x will certainly be greater than 0. The last line of code executes regardless of x's value, so you should mark (B) with a "T". Choice C subtracts 4 from x, then multiplies x by 2. You do not know if x is positive, so you should mark C with an "F". You know that you need to have two choices marked "F" and two choices marked "T", so there is no need to work through Choice D, unless you want to check your work. It must be true.

OUTPUT/STATE QUESTIONS

OUTPUT/STATE questions are usually programming or algorithm questions that ask you to identify the result after following a series of steps. You should be very careful about reading every line of code or step, watching out for "if" statements and making sure you iterate through loops the appropriate number of times. Be sure to utilize the Reference Sheet.

For example:

5. Consider the code segment below:

```
REPEAT UNTIL (NOT CAN_MOVE(right))
{
  IF(CAN_MOVE (forward))
  {
    MOVE_FORWARD()
  }
  IF(NOT CAN_MOVE (forward))
  {
    ROTATE_RIGHT ()
    ROTATE_RIGHT ()
    MOVE_FORWARD()
  }
}
```

For the following initial situation, what will be the final position and direction of the robot after the code is executed?

(A)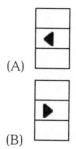

(B)

(C) The program terminates when the robot attempts to move off the grid.

(D) There is an infinite loop.

ANSWER: C. The robot attempts to move off the grid after turning around. The first line of the code tells you that you are in a REPEAT UNTIL loop. Every time you reach the end of the loop's curly brace, recheck the condition to see if it's true. Once it's true, you can stop iterating though the loop.

1st iteration: The robot can move right, so we enter the loop. The first "if" statement checks to see if we can move forward. We cannot, so we don't execute the code in its curly braces. The next "if" statement checks if we cannot move forward. We cannot, so we execute the steps in the curly braces. After rotating twice, we attempt to move forward, but attempt to move off the grid, which terminates the program.

Part II

A Review of AP® Computer Science Principles

1

Big Idea 1: Creativity

Overview

Computing is a creative activity.

The AP® Computer Science Principles Course emphasizes creativity in computing. The Essential Knowledge statements for this Big Idea are assessed in the two though-course Performance Tasks. You should practice for these Performance Tasks before attempting them, using the computational tools you learn through the course. Familiarity with the tasks and the reflection questions, and feedback from practice tasks, will help you create relevant artifacts which extend traditional forms of human expression and experience.

Since Essential Knowledge for this Big Idea is assessed on the through-course performance tasks only, and not on the written multiple-choice exam, this chapter does not include any practice multiple-choice questions. However, below is the outline of all Learning Objectives and Essential Knowledge statements related to Big Idea 1: Creativity. Use these Learning Objective statements to understand what you are expected to be able to do by the end of the course with respect to Creativity. The Essential Knowledge statements provide specific facts or content that you are expected to know in demonstrating your understanding of the Learning Objectives.

LEARNING OBJECTIVES AND ESSENTIAL KNOWLEDGE STATEMENTS

LEARNING OBJECTIVES	ESSENTIAL KNOWLEDGE
LO 1.1.1 Apply a creative development process when creating computational artifacts.	**EK 1.1.1A** A creative process in the development of a computational artifact can include, but is not limited to, employing nontraditional, non-prescribed techniques; the use of novel combinations of artifacts, tools, and techniques; and the exploration of personal curiosities. **EK 1.1.1B** Creating computational artifacts employs an iterative and often exploratory process to translate ideas into tangible form.
LO 1.2.1 Create a computational artifact for creative expression.	**EK 1.2.1A** A computational artifact is something created by a human using a computer and can be, but is not limited to, a program, an image, an audio, a video, a presentation, or a Web page file. **EK 1.2.1B** Creating computational artifacts requires understanding of and use of software tools and services. **EK 1.2.1C** Computing tools and techniques are used to create computational artifacts and can include, but are not limited to, programming integrated development environments (IDEs), spreadsheets, three-dimensional (3-D) printers, or text editors. **EK 1.2.1D** A creatively developed computational artifact can be created by using non-traditional, non-prescribed computing techniques. **EK 1.2.1E** Creative expressions in a computational artifact can reflect personal expressions of ideas or interests.

LEARNING OBJECTIVES	ESSENTIAL KNOWLEDGE
LO 1.2.2 Create a computational artifact using computing tools and techniques to solve a problem.	**EK 1.2.2A** Computing tools and techniques can enhance the process of finding a solution to a problem. **EK 1.2.2B** A creative development process for creating computational artifacts can be used to solve problems when traditional or prescribed computing techniques are not effective.
LO 1.2.3 Create a new computational artifact by combining or modifying existing artifacts.	**EK 1.2.3A** Creating computational artifacts can be done by combining and modifying existing artifacts or by creating new artifacts. **EK 1.2.3B** Computation facilitates the creation and modification of computational artifacts with enhanced detail and precision. **EK 1.2.3C** Combining or modifying existing artifacts can show personal expression of ideas.
LO 1.2.4 Collaborate in the creation of computational artifacts.	**EK 1.2.4A** A collaboratively created computational artifact reflects effort by more than one person. **EK 1.2.4B** Effective collaborative teams consider the use of online collaborative tools. **EK 1.2.4C** Effective collaborative teams practice interpersonal communication, consensus building, conflict resolution, and negotiation. **EK 1.2.4D** Effective collaboration strategies enhance performance. **EK 1.2.4E** Collaboration facilitates the application of multiple perspectives (including sociocultural perspectives) and diverse talents and skills in developing computational artifacts.

LEARNING OBJECTIVES	ESSENTIAL KNOWLEDGE
LO 1.2.4 (cont'd) Collaborate in the creation of computational artifacts.	**EK 1.2.4F** A collaboratively created computational artifact can reflect personal expressions of ideas.
LO 1.2.5 Analyze the correctness, usability, functionality, and suitability of computational artifacts.	**EK 1.2.5A** The context in which an artifact is used determines the correctness, usability, functionality, and suitability of the artifact. **EK 1.2.5B** A computational artifact may have weaknesses, mistakes, or errors depending on the type of artifact. **EK 1.2.5C** The functionality of a computational artifact may be related to how it is used or perceived. **EK 1.2.5D** The suitability (or appropriateness) of a computational artifact may be related to how it Is used or perceived.
LO 1.3.1 Use computing tools and techniques for creative expression.	**EK 1.3.1A** Creating digital effects, images, audio, video, and animations has transformed industries. **EK 1.3.1B** Digital audio and music can be created by synthesizing sounds, sampling existing audio and music, and recording and manipulating sounds, including layering and looping. **EK 1.3.1C** Digital images can be created by generating pixel patterns, manipulating existing digital images, or combining images. **EK 1.3.1D** Digital effects and animation can be created by using existing software or modified software that includes functionality to implement the effects and animations.

LEARNING OBJECTIVES	ESSENTIAL KNOWLEDGE
LO 1.3.1 (cont'd) Use computing tools and techniques for creative expression.	**EK 1.3.1E** Computing enables creative exploration of both real and virtual phenomena.

2

BIG IDEA 2:
ABSTRACTION

OVERVIEW

Abstraction reduces information and detail to facilitate focus on relevant concepts.

Abstraction involves looking at the bigger picture to better understand a concept. For example, when we write code in a programming language, we use procedures that already exist, like PRINT. We do not need to concern ourselves with the details of how those procedures were written, we just need to know how to use them. In this course, you will work with and learn to recognize abstraction as a process, a strategy, and a result as you engage with computational problems and systems. Questions from Big Idea 2 include base conversions, logic gates, and questions about models and simulations.

LEARNING OBJECTIVES AND ESSENTIAL KNOWLEDGE STATEMENTS

LEARNING OBJECTIVES	ESSENTIAL KNOWLEDGE
LO 2.1.1 Describe the variety of abstractions used to represent data.	**EK 2.1.1A** Digital data is represented by abstractions at different levels.
	EK 2.1.1B At the lowest level, all digital data are represented by bits.

LEARNING OBJECTIVES	ESSENTIAL KNOWLEDGE
LO 2.1.1 (cont'd) Describe the variety of abstractions used to represent data.	**EK 2.1.1C** At a higher level, bits are grouped to represent abstractions, including but not limited to numbers, characters, and color. **EK 2.1.1D** Number bases, including binary, decimal, and hexadecimal, are used to represent and investigate digital data. **EK 2.1.1E** At one of the lowest levels of abstraction, digital data is represented in binary (base 2) using only combinations of the digits zero and one. EXCLUSION STATEMENT (for EK 2.1.1E) Two's complement conversions are beyond the scope of this course and the AP® Exam. **EK 2.1.1F** Hexadecimal (base 16) is used to represent digital data because hexadecimal representation uses fewer digits than binary. **EK 2.1.1G** Numbers can be converted from any base to any other base.
LO 2.1.2 Explain how binary sequences are used to represent digital data.	**EK 2.1.2A** A finite representation is used to model the infinite mathematical concept of a number. EXCLUSION STATEMENT (for EK 2.1.2A) Binary representations of scientific notation are beyond the scope of this course and the AP® Exam. **EK 2.1.2B** In many programming languages, the fixed number of bits used to represent characters or integers limits the range of integer values and mathematical operations; this limitation can result in overflow or other errors.

LEARNING OBJECTIVES	ESSENTIAL KNOWLEDGE
LO 2.1.2 (cont'd) Explain how binary sequences are used to represent digital data.	EXCLUSION STATEMENT (for EK 2.1.2B) Range limitations of any one language, compiler, or architecture are beyond the scope of this course and the AP® Exam. **EK 2.1.2C** In many programming languages, the fixed number of bits used to represent real numbers (as floating-point numbers) limits the range of floating-point values and mathematical operations; this limitation can result in round off and other errors. **EK 2.1.2D** The interpretation of a binary sequence depends on how it is used. **EK 2.1.2E** A sequence of bits may represent instructions or data. **EK 2.1.2F** A sequence of bits may represent different types of data in different contexts.
LO 2.2.1 Develop an abstraction when writing a program or creating other computational artifacts.	**EK 2.2.1A** The process of developing an abstraction involves removing detail and generalizing functionality. **EK 2.2.1B** An abstraction extracts common features from specific examples in order to generalize concepts. **EK 2.2.1C** An abstraction generalizes functionality with input parameters that allow software reuse. EXCLUSION STATEMENT (for EK 2.2.1C) An understanding of the difference between value and reference parameters is beyond the scope of this course and the AP® Exam.

LEARNING OBJECTIVES	ESSENTIAL KNOWLEDGE
LO 2.2.2 Use multiple levels of abstraction to write programs.	**EK 2.2.2A** Software is developed using multiple levels of abstractions, such as constants, expressions, statements, procedures, and libraries. **EK 2.2.2B** Being aware of and using multiple levels of abstractions in developing programs help to more effectively apply available resources and tools to solve problems.
LO 2.2.3 Identify multiple levels of abstractions that are used when writing programs.	**EK 2.2.3A** Different programming languages offer different levels of abstraction. EXCLUSION STATEMENT (for EK 2.2.3A) Knowledge of the abstraction capabilities of all programming languages is beyond the scope of this course and the AP® Exam. **EK 2.2.3B** High-level programming languages provide more abstractions for the programmer and make it easier for people to read and write a program. **EK 2.2.3C** Code in a programming language is often translated into code in another (lower-level) language to be executed on a computer. **EK 2.2.3D** In an abstraction hierarchy, higher levels of abstraction (the most general concepts) would be placed toward the top and lower-level abstractions (the more specific concepts) toward the bottom. **EK 2.2.3E** Binary data is processed by physical layers of computing hardware, including gates, chips, and components.

LEARNING OBJECTIVES	ESSENTIAL KNOWLEDGE
LO 2.2.3 (cont'd) Identify multiple levels of abstractions that are used when writing programs.	**EK 2.2.3F** A logic gate is a hardware abstraction that is modeled by a Boolean function. EXCLUSION STATEMENT (for 2.2.3F) Memorization of specific gate visual representations is beyond the scope of this course and the AP® Exam. **EK 2.2.3G** A chip is an abstraction composed of low-level components and circuits that perform a specific function. **EK 2.2.3H** A hardware component can be low level like a transistor or high level like a video card. **EK 2.2.3I** Hardware is built using multiple levels of abstractions, such as transistors, logic gates, chips, memory, motherboards, special purpose cards, and storage devices. **EK 2.2.3J** Applications and systems are designed, developed, and analyzed using levels of hardware, software, and conceptual abstractions. **EK 2.2.3K** Lower-level abstractions can be combined to make higher-level abstractions, such as short message services (SMS) or email messages, images, audio files, and videos.
LO 2.3.1 Use models and simulations to represent phenomena.	**EK 2.3.1A** Models and simulations are simplified representations of more complex objects of phenomena. **EK 2.3.1B** Models may use different abstractions or levels of abstraction depending on the objects or phenomena being posed.

LEARNING OBJECTIVES	ESSENTIAL KNOWLEDGE
LO 2.3.1 (cont'd) Use models and simulations to represent phenomena.	**EK 2.3.1C** Models often omit unnecessary features of the objects or phenomena that are being modeled. **EK 2.3.1D** Simulations mimic real-world events without the cost or danger of building and testing the phenomena in the real world.
LO 2.3.2 Use models and simulations to formulate, refine, and test hypotheses.	**EK 2.3.2A** Models and simulations facilitate the formulation and refinement of hypotheses related to the objects of phenomena under consideration. **EK 2.3.2B** Hypotheses are formulated to explain the objects or phenomena being modeled. **EK 2.3.2C** Hypotheses are refined by examining the insights that models and simulations provide into the objects or phenomena. **EK 2.3.2D** The results of simulations may generate new knowledge and new hypotheses related to the phenomena being modeled. **EK 2.3.2E** Simulations allow hypotheses to be tested without the constraints of the real world. **EK 2.3.2F** Simulations can facilitate extensive and rapid testing of models. **EK 2.3.2G** The time required for simulations is impacted by the level of detail and quality of the models and the software and hardware used for the simulation. **EK 2.3.2H** Rapid and extensive testing allows models to be changed to accurately reflect the objects or phenomena being modeled.

Practice Questions

1. Which of the following are considered abstractions in the use of cell phones?
   I. A mobile application written in a programming language.
   II. The phone's hundreds of millions of transistors act like switches to represent 1s and 0s.
   III. The icons on the screen representing applications.

   (A) I only
   (B) II only
   (C) I and II
   (D) I, II, and III

2. Numbers can be represented in multiple bases. For example, in the octal system we can represent 8 digits. Numbers in octal can be expressed by writing the number followed by a subscript 8 indicating that the number is an octal digit. Convert 24_8 to decimal.
   (A) 6
   (B) 14
   (C) 20
   (D) 160

3. What base could the number 18 be in?
   I. octal (base 8)
   II. decimal (base 10)
   III. hexadecimal (base 16)

   (A) I and II
   (B) I and III
   (C) II and III
   (D) I, II, and III

4. One way or representing colors in HTML is in hexadecimal, such as #FFEB5A or as an RGB value, such as (255, 235, 90) which expresses the red, green, and blue values in decimal. The first two digits in the hexadecimal code correspond to the decimal representation of the red value, the next two digits to the green value, and the last two to the blue value. Which of the following hexadecimal values corresponds to the RGB value (0, 255, 213)?
   (A) #00FFD5
   (B) #FF00D5
   (C) #00FFE5
   (D) #FF00E5

5. Put the following in order, from least to greatest: 100_{10}, 1011010_2, $6A_{16}$.
   (A) 100_{10}, 1011010_2, $6A_{16}$
   (B) 1011010_2, $6A_{16}$, 100_{10}
   (C) $6A_{16}$, 100_{10}, 1011010_2
   (D) 1011010_2, 100_{10}, $6A_{16}$

6. Which of the following is not a common number system utilized in the representation of data?
   (A) base 2
   (B) base 10
   (C) base 16
   (D) base 32

7. Which of the following procedures will correctly remove all multiples of num from numList?

   I.
   ```
   PROCEDURE removeMultiples(num, numList)
   {
       FOR EACH item IN numList
       {
           IF (num MOD item = 0)
           {
               REMOVE (numList, item)
           }
       }
   }
   ```

   II.
   ```
   PROCEDURE removeMultiples(num, numList)
   {
       n ← 1
       REPEAT LENGTH (numList) TIMES
       {
           n ← 1
           IF (numList[n]  MOD num = 0)
           {
               REMOVE (numList, item)
           }
           n ← n + 1
       }
   }
   ```

   III.
   ```
   PROCEDURE removeMultiples(num, numList)
   {
       n ← 1
       FOR EACH item IN numList
       {
           IF (num MOD item = 0)
           {
               REMOVE (numList, n)
           }
           n ← n + 1
       }
   }
   ```

   (A) I only
   (B) III only
   (C) I and II
   (D) II and III

8. A programmer has a choice between a higher-level and a lower-level programming language to use. Which should she choose, and why?
    (A) The higher-level language, because the language itself will be less complex, and there will be fewer errors.
    (B) The lower-level language, because it offers more flexibility for complex programs.
    (C) It depends on her needs, as a higher level language will be less complex, but will not allow as much freedom as a lower-level language.
    (D) Either language, because both languages will be converted to a lower level language to be executed on the computer.

9. Consider the program displayHighway, which displays several cars on a highway. The program includes the following procedures: displayAntennas(), displayWheels(), displayWindows(), displayCar(), displayRoad(). Which of the following is an appropriate visualization of the program's abstraction hierarchy?

(A)

displayRoad()
displayAntennas(), displayWheels(), displayWindows()
displayCar()

(B)

displayCar()
displayAntennas(), displayWheels(), displayWindows()
displayRoad()

(C)

displayAntennas(), displayWheels(), displayWindows()
displayCar()
displayRoad()

(D)

displayRoad()
displayCar()
displayAntennas(), displayWheels(), displayWindows()

10. Consider the goal of flipping two fair coins simultaneously three times and displaying the number of times both coins land on heads. Which of the following code segments can be used to accomplish that goal?

(A)
```
count ← 0
REPEAT 3 TIMES
{
    IF (RANDOM(0,1) = RANDOM(0,1))
    {
        count ← count + 1
    }
}
DISPLAY count
```

(B)
```
count ← 0
REPEAT 3 TIMES
{
    IF (RANDOM(1,2) = RANDOM(1,2))
    {
        count ← count + 1
    }
}
DISPLAY count
```

(C)
```
REPEAT 3 TIMES
{
    count ← 0
    IF (RANDOM(0,1) = RANDOM(0,1))
    {
        count ← count + 1
    }
}
DISPLAY count
```

(D)
```
count ← 0
REPEAT 3 TIMES
{
    IF (RANDOM(0,1) = RANDOM(1,2))
    {
        count ← count + 1
    }
}
DISPLAY count
```

Answers

1. **Answer: D.** I, II, and III are all examples of abstractions in the use of cell phones.

Learning Objectives	Essential Knowledge
LO 2.1.1 Describe the variety of abstractions used to represent data.	**EK 2.1.1A** Digital data is represented by abstractions at different levels. **EK 2.1.1B** At the lowest level, all digital data are represented by bits. **EK 2.1.1E** At one of the lowest levels of abstraction, digital data is represented in binary (base 2) using only combinations of the digits zero and one.

2. **Answer: C.** Converting 24_8 from octal to decimal yields: $2 * 8^1 + 4 * 8^0 = 20$.

Learning Objectives	Essential Knowledge
LO 2.1.1 Describe the variety of abstractions used to represent data.	**EK 2.1.1G** Numbers can be converted from any base to any other base.

3. **Answer: C.** 8 is not a digit in octal, but 1 and 8 are both digits in decimal and hexadecimal.

Learning Objectives	Essential Knowledge
LO 2.1.1 Describe the variety of abstractions used to represent data.	**EK 2.1.1A** Digital data is represented by abstractions at different levels. **EK 2.1.1D** Number bases, including binary, decimal, and hexadecimal, are used to represent and investigate digital data. **EK 2.1.1E** At one of the lowest levels of abstraction, digital data is represented in binary (base 2) using only combinations of the digits zero and one. **EK 2.1.1F** Hexadecimal (base 16) is used to represent digital data because hexadecimal representation uses fewer digits than binary. **EK 2.1.1G** Numbers can be converted from any base to any other base.

4. **Answer: A.** The ordered triplet needs to be converted from decimal values to hexadecimal. 0_{10} is 00_{16}, 255_{10} is FF_{16}, and 213_{10} is $D5_{16}$.

Learning Objectives	Essential Knowledge
LO 2.1.1 Describe the variety of abstractions used to represent data.	EK 2.1.1A Digital data is represented by abstractions at different levels.
	EK 2.1.1B At the lowest level, all digital data are represented by bits.
	EK 2.1.1C At a higher level, bits are grouped to represent abstractions, including but not limited to numbers, characters, and color.
	EK 2.1.1D Number bases, including binary, decimal, and hexadecimal, are used to represent and investigate digital data.

5. **Answer: D.** Compare the values by writing all of them in decimal. The values, in decimal, are $1011010_2 = 90$, $100_{10} = 100$, and $6A_{16} = 106$.

Learning Objectives	Essential Knowledge
LO 2.1.1 Describe the variety of abstractions used to represent data.	EK 2.1.1B At the lowest level, all digital data are represented by bits.
	EK 2.1.1D Number bases, including binary, decimal, and hexadecimal, are used to represent and investigate digital data.
	EK 2.1.1E At one of the lowest levels of abstraction, digital data is represented in binary (base 2) using only combinations of the digits zero and one.
	EK 2.1.1F Hexadecimal (base 16) is used to represent digital data because hexadecimal representation uses fewer digits than binary.
	EK 2.1.1G Numbers can be converted from any base to any other base.

6. **Answer: D.** While base 2, base 10, and base 16 are commonly utilized in computing, base 32 is not.

Learning Objectives	Essential Knowledge
LO 2.1.1 Describe the variety of abstractions used to represent data.	**EK 2.1.1A** Digital data is represented by abstractions at different levels.
	EK 2.1.1C At a higher level, bits are grouped to represent abstractions, including but not limited to numbers, characters, and color.
	EK 2.1.1D Number bases, including binary, decimal, and hexadecimal, are used to represent and investigate digital data.
	EK 2.1.1E At one of the lowest levels of abstraction, digital data is represented in binary (base 2) using only combinations of the digits zero and one.
	EK 2.1.1F Hexadecimal (base 16) is used to represent digital data because hexadecimal representation uses fewer digits than binary.
	EK 2.1.1G Numbers can be converted from any base to any other base.

7. **Answer: B.** Only the procedure described in Option III removes the correct value at the correct index.

Learning Objectives	Essential Knowledge
LO 2.2.1 Develop an abstraction when writing a program or creating other computational artifacts.	**EK 2.2.1A** The process of developing an abstraction involves removing detail and generalizing functionality.
	EK 2.2.1B An abstraction extracts common features from specific examples in order to generalize concepts.
	EK 2.2.1C An abstraction generalizes functionality with input parameters that allow software reuse.
LO 5.5.1 Employ appropriate mathematical and logical concepts in programming.	**EK 5.5.1E** Logical concepts and Boolean algebra are fundamental to programming.

8. **Answer: C**. The decision should be based on the specific situation. She needs to use the language that gives her the appropriate complexity and flexibility to solve the problem at hand.

Learning Objectives	Essential Knowledge
LO 2.2.3 Identify multiple levels of abstractions that are used when writing programs.	**EK 2.2.3A** Different programming languages offer different levels of abstraction.
	EK 2.2.3B High-level programming languages provide more abstractions for the programmer and make it easier for people to read and write a program.
	EK 2.2.3C Code in a programming language is often translated into code in another (lower level) language to be executed on a computer.

9. **Answer: D**. The simplest items are at the bottom, which make up the car, and the road will contain several cars.

Learning Objectives	Essential Knowledge
LO 2.2.3 Identify multiple levels of abstractions that are used when writing programs.	**EK 2.2.3D** In an abstraction hierarchy, higher levels of abstraction (the most general concepts) would be placed toward the top and lower level abstractions (the more specific concepts) toward the bottom.

10. **Answer: D**. We can assume that 1 is heads, so each coin has a 50% chance of getting heads.

Learning Objectives	Essential Knowledge
LO 2.3.1 Use models and simulations to represent phenomena.	**EK 2.3.1A** Models and simulations are simplified representations of more complex objects of phenomena.
	EK 2.3.1B Models may use different abstractions or levels of abstraction depending on the objects or phenomena being posed.
	EK 2.3.1C Models often omit unnecessary features of the objects or phenomena that are being modeled.
LO 5.2.1 Develop a correct program to solve problems.	**EK 5.2.1B** Program instructions are executed sequentially.
	EK 5.2.1C Program instructions may involve variables that are initialized, updated, read, and written.

3

BIG IDEA 3:
DATA AND INFORMATION

OVERVIEW

Data and information facilitate the creation of knowledge.

Data is used to create new information. Using computational tools and techniques, we can manipulate raw data to understand things in new ways. As an information society, while we are now able to gather, store and process incredibly vast amounts of raw data, the computing power of today allows us to make connections that would never have been found just a few years ago. Questions from Big Idea 3 include questions about sorting, storing, and working with data, as well as the trade-offs that may arise in the computational manipulation of data. Big Idea 3 is also assessed in the Impact Performance task.

LEARNING OBJECTIVES AND ESSENTIAL KNOWLEDGE STATEMENTS

LEARNING OBJECTIVES	ESSENTIAL KNOWLEDGE
LO 3.1.1 Find patterns and test hypotheses about digitally processed information to gain insight and knowledge.	**EK 3.1.1A** Computers are used in an iterative and interactive way when processing digital information to gain insight and knowledge. **EK 3.1.1B** Digital information can be filtered and cleaned by using computers to process information.

LEARNING OBJECTIVES	ESSENTIAL KNOWLEDGE
LO 3.1.1 (cont'd) Find patterns and test hypotheses about digitally processed information to gain insight and knowledge.	**EK 3.1.1C** Combining data sources, clustering data, and data classification are part of the process of using computers to process information. **EK 3.1.1D** Insight and knowledge can be obtained from translating and transforming digitally represented information. **EK 3.1.1E** Patterns can emerge when data is transformed using computational tools.
LO 3.1.2 Collaborate when processing information to gain insight and knowledge.	**EK 3.1.2A** Collaboration is an important part of solving data-driven problems. **EK 3.1.2B** Collaboration facilitates solving computational problems by applying multiple perspectives, experiences, and skill sets. **EK 3.1.2C** Communication between participants working on data-driven problems gives rise to enhanced insights and knowledge. **EK 3.1.2D** Collaboration in developing hypotheses and questions, and in testing hypotheses and answering questions, about data helps participants gain insight and knowledge. **EK 3.1.2E** Collaborating face-to-face and using online collaborative tools can facilitate processing information to gain insight and knowledge. **EK 3.1.2F** Investigating large data sets collaboratively can lead to insight and knowledge not obtained when working alone.

LEARNING OBJECTIVES	ESSENTIAL KNOWLEDGE
LO 3.1.3 Explain the insight and knowledge gained from digitally processed data by using appropriate visualizations, notations, and precise language.	**EK 3.1.3A** Visualization tools and software can communicate information about data. **EK 3.1.3B** Tables, diagrams, and textual displays can be used in communicating insight and knowledge gained from data. **EK 3.1.3C** Summaries of data analyzed computationally can be effective in communicating insight and knowledge gained from digitally represented information. **EK 3.1.3D** Transforming information can be effective in communicating knowledge gained from data. **EK 3.1.3E** Interactivity with data is an aspect of communicating.
LO 3.2.1 Extract information from data to discover and explain connections or trends.	**EK 3.2.1A** Large data sets provide opportunities and challenges for extracting information and knowledge. **EK 3.2.1B** Large data sets provide opportunities for identifying trends, making connections in data, and solving problems. **EK 3.2.1C** Computing tools facilitate the discovery of connections in information within large data sets. **EK 3.2.1D** Search tools are essential for efficiently finding information. **EK 3.2.1E** Information filtering systems are important tools for finding information and recognizing patterns in the information.

LEARNING OBJECTIVES	ESSENTIAL KNOWLEDGE
LO 3.2.1 (cont'd) Extract information from data to discover and explain connections or trends.	**EK 3.2.1F** Software tools, including spreadsheets and databases, help to efficiently organize and find trends in information. EXCLUSION STATEMENT (for EK 3.2.1F): Students are not expected to know specific formulas or options available in spreadsheet or database software packages. **EK 3.2.1G** Metadata is data about data. **EK 3.2.1H** Metadata can be descriptive data about an image, a Web page, or other complex objects. **EK 3.2.1I** Metadata can increase the effective use of data or data sets by providing additional information about various aspects of that data.
LO 3.2.2 Determine how large data sets impact the use of computational processes to discover information and knowledge.	**EK 3.2.2A** Large data sets include data such as transactions, measurements, texts, sounds, images, and videos. **EK 3.2.2B** The storing, processing, and curating of large data sets is challenging. **EK 3.2.2C** Structuring large data sets for analysis can be challenging. **EK 3.2.2D** Maintaining privacy of large data sets containing personal information can be challenging. **EK 3.2.2E** Scalability of systems is an important consideration when data sets are large. **EK 3.2.2F** The size or scale of a system that stores data affects how the data set is used.

LEARNING OBJECTIVES	ESSENTIAL KNOWLEDGE
LO 3.2.2 (cont'd) Determine how large data sets impact the use of computational processes to discover information and knowledge.	**EK 3.2.2G** The effective use of large data sets requires computational solutions. **EK 3.2.2H** Analytical techniques to store, manage, transmit, and process data sets change as the size of data sets scale.
LO 3.3.1 Analyze how data representation, storage, security, and transmission of data involve computational manipulation of information.	**EK 3.3.1A** Digital data representations involve trade-offs related to storage, security, and privacy concerns. **EK 3.3.1B** Security concerns engender trade-offs in storing and transmitting information. **EK 3.3.1C** There are trade-offs is using lossy and lossless compression techniques for storing and transmitting data. **EK 3.3.1D** Lossless data compression reduces the number of bits stored or transmitted but allows complete reconstruction of the original data. **EK3.3.1E** Lossy data compression can significantly reduce the number of bits stored or transmitted at the cost of being able to reconstruct only an approximation of the original data. **EK 3.3.1F** Security and privacy concerns arise with data containing personal information. **EK 3.3.1G** Data is stored in many formats depending on its characteristics (e.g., size and intended use). **EK 3.3.1H** The choice of storage media affects both the methods and costs of manipulating the data it contains. **EK 3.3.1I** Reading data and updating data have different storage requirements.

Practice Questions

1. Big data is more readily available today than it has ever been in the past. It is being created, accessed, and manipulated by professionals and amateurs alike. Which of the following statements below accurately describes the relationship between reading data and updating data?
   (A) Reading data and updating data have the same storage requirements.
   (B) Reading data requires less storage than updating data.
   (C) There is no relationship between reading and updating data.
   (D) Reading data requires more storage than updating data.

2. A school sports reporter has been given access to a data set of sports statistics that she is going to analyze for a research project. Which of the following types of software can she NOT use to organize and analyze the data?
   (A) Spreadsheet software
   (B) Webpage Software
   (C) Database software
   (D) Visualization Software

3. A librarian gathered data to analyze the ebooks that were borrowed from the library in the past six months. An ebook was listed in the data every time it was borrowed. the following data was collected for each ebook:
   ▦ Author
   ▦ Ebook title
   ▦ Genre
   The librarian wants to find the number of **unique** books read in the mystery genre. Of the algorithms below, which can the librarian use to find the number of **unique** books read in the mystery genre? Select <u>two</u> answers.

   (A) Filter the data by creating a list of ebooks only in the mystery genre. Sort the list of mystery books by title. Iterate through the sorted list. If an ebook is the same as the previous ebook on the list, delete it from the list. Find the size of the list.
   (B) Filter the data by creating a list of ebooks only in the mystery genre. Sort the list of mystery books by author. Iterate through the sorted list. If an author of an ebook is the same as that of the previous author on the list, delete it from the list. Find the size of the list.
   (C) Create a new list of the data sorted by ebook title. Iterate through the sorted list. Every time an ebook is the same as the previous ebook, delete the duplicate ebook from the list. Set a counter to 0.Iterate through the remaining list of ebooks. Each time mystery is listed, increment the counter by 1.

(D) Create a new list of the data sorted by author. Iterate through the sorted list. Every time an author is the same as the previous author, delete the duplicate author and accompanying data from the list. Set a counter to 0. Iterate through the remaining list of authors. Each time mystery is listed, increment the counter by 1.

4. A football manager is preparing his roster for the new season. He has a database of players that includes the following:
   ▪ Names
   ▪ Jersey numbers
   ▪ Jersey Sizes
   ▪ Position
   ▪ Age
   ▪ Weight
   He wants to sort and filter the players in various ways for ordering of supplies and other game preparations. He has two languages he would like to use; one is blocks-based, and the other is text-based. Which should he choose and why?

   (A) Text-based, because text-based languages are traditionally better with filtering and sorting data.
   (B) Blocks-based, because blocks-based languages are traditionally better with filtering and sorting data.
   (C) Either option is acceptable, because the numerical values associated with the data are small enough not to cause run-time exceptions.
   (D) Ether option is acceptable, because languages are nearly equivalent in terms of being able to express any algorithm.

5. In order to get more students interested in art, an art professor is planning a week-long "course on the road" entitled Teenage Mutant Ninja Artists. The course will travel around the northeastern United States exposing the students to the work of Michelangelo, Donatello, Rafael, and Leonardo da Vinci. The professor has access to a large database of museums that house various works from the artists. The database includes the name of the artist, the name of the piece, the type of piece, and the name of the museum. If the professor wants to ensure that the students are exposed to the maximum number of works from each artist, how should they build their query of the database?

(A) The professor should run a query that returns a ranked list of the total number of pieces from the four artists at each museum. The professor can then query that data to create an ordered list of the names of each work by artist and museum. They can then determine which museums have the most unique set of works from all four artists.

(B) The professor should run a query that returns a ranked list of the total number of pieces from the four artists at each museum. The professor can then query that data to create an ordered list of how many works are at each museum by each artist.

(C) The professor should run a query that returns a list of the total number of pieces from the four artists at each museum. The professor can then query that data to generate a travel itinerary based on the proximity of the museum and number of works by artists.

(D) The professor should run a query that returns a list of works by artist. That data can be queried to generate a report that matches the list of works to the locations of the museums. The professor can then make a decision on the itinerary they wish to create to allow the students to experience as many works as possible.

6. A movie streaming site collects the following data from all of its subscribers:
   ▨ Geo-location of the viewer
   ▨ User device information
   ▨ Time of day/night the content is accessed
   ▨ When the user pauses and restarts the content
   Based on this data alone, which of the following is NOT true? (Assume there are not multiple user profiles available.)

(A) The site might make different recommendations when you log in on your laptop versus when you log in on your tablet.

(B) The site knows precisely how many people are watching content at a given location.

(C) The site can determine the point during content viewing when the user is likely to navigate away from the site, and offer suggestions for different content.

(D) The site can determine that TV shows are watched during the week while movies are watched on the weekends.

7. When scientists make discoveries, the expectation of the scientific community is that they share their data with their peers so that their findings can be recreated and verified. However, that is often easier said than done. Which of the following is NOT a reason why scientists may be unable to share their data?
   (A) Much of the scientific data is not in digital format and the originating scientist has no responsibility to digitize it for peer review.
   (B) There is no central, storage space where data can be kept and easily accessed by other scientists.
   (C) For many fields, there is no uniform methodology for how to record and describe data.
   (D) Often times, scientists overlook the need to include metadata in the data they make available.

8. All file types include some form of metadata. Which of the following accurately describe the metadata that might be found in each file type?
   I. Digital image: size of the image, color depth, image resolution, date the image was created, location where image was created.
   II. Text document: content in the document, copy of the file, other content imported into the document.
   III. Web page: description of page content, key words that reference content and assist in web searches.

   (A) III only
   (B) I and II only
   (C) I and III only
   (D) All of the above

9. In the educational world teachers present data and information and students process it to gain the desired knowledge. In the digital world, there are search engines, wiki pages, and the like that provide access to information that people can use to gain knowledge. Even in our daily lives we take in data and information and convert that to knowledge. The field is new and growing; what is it called when we transform this data/information into knowledge?
   (A) Knowledge acquisition
   (B) Data transference
   (C) Wisdom inferencing
   (D) Information alchemy

10. The digital landscape has made large data sets more accessible than they have ever been before. Data is the most valuable resource for researchers and the sheer amount of it is changing the way research is done. While big data is often seen as a positive, researchers must also be wary of some aspects of it. Which of the following are challenges for researchers working with big data?

I. The collection of the data is more important than how the researcher is going to use it.

II. Because of the amounts of data present, many researchers look for trends that support their hypotheses rather than let the data lead them.

III. Large data sets require special analytical tools (servers and other equipment) that some researchers may not have and/or may not realize they need to use.

IV. New computational techniques are not keeping up with the growing number and size of data sets available.

V. Large data sets usually come from multiple sources which means that collection techniques may have differed. A researcher not taking this into consideration may come to incorrect conclusions.

(A) I, II, and IV only
(B) I, II, III, and V only
(C) II, III, and V only
(D) All of the above.

Answers

1. **Answer: B**. Reading data requires less storage because there is not active usage of storage other than RAM. Updating data requires that the storage be scalable and have the capacity to accommodate the additional/updated data.

Learning Objectives	Essential Knowledge
LO 3.3.1 Analyze how data representation, storage, security, and transmission of data involve computational manipulation of information.	**EK 3.3.1I** Reading data and updating data have different storage requirements.

2. **Answer: B**. While she could use webpage software to display the data and the trends and information it conveys, web page software in and of itself will not do any analysis or organization of the data.

Learning Objectives	Essential Knowledge
LO 3.2.1 Extract information from data to discover and explain connections and trends.	**EK 3.2.1F** Software tools, including spreadsheets and databases help to efficiently organize and find trends in information.

3. **Answers: A, C**. Choice A filters the data and eliminates repetitions from the list. Choice C counts non-duplicated values.

Learning Objectives	Essential Knowledge
LO 3.1.1 Find patterns and test hypotheses about digitally processed information to gain insight and knowledge.	**EK 3.1.1B** Digital information can be filtered and cleaned by using computers to process information.
LO 4.1.1 Develop an algorithm for implementation in a program.	**EK 4.1.1H** Different algorithms can be developed to solve the same problem.

4. **Answer: D**. The manager should use the code he is comfortable with, as the languages are most likely equivalent.

Learning Objectives	Essential Knowledge
LO 3.2.1 Extract information from data to discover and explain connections and trends.	**EK 3.2.1F** Software tools, including spreadsheets and databases, help to efficiently organize and find trends in information.
LO 4.1.2 Express an algorithm in a language.	**EK 4.1.2H** Nearly all programming languages are equivalent in terms of being able to express any algorithm.

5. **Answer: A.** Choice A is the only query that will return a list that allows the professor to make an accurate determination of which museum visits will let them see the most works of all the artists. Answer B only returns a list but it does not include unique locations. Options C and D both reference museum location, which is not available in the database.

Learning Objectives	Essential Knowledge
LO 3.1.1 Find patterns and test hypotheses about digitally processed information to gain insight and knowledge.	EK 3.1.1A Computers are used in an iterative and interactive way when processing digital information to gain insight and knowledge.

6. **Answer: B.** Although the site can track starts, pauses, and re-starts, they cannot know the number of people that may be watching the content at a single location.

Learning Objectives	Essential Knowledge
LO 3.1.1 Find patterns and test hypotheses about digitally processed information to gain insight and knowledge.	EK 3.1.1A Computers are used in an iterative and interactive way when processing digital information to gain insight and knowledge.
	EK 3.1.1B Digital information can be filtered and cleaned by using computers to process information.
	EK 3.1.1D Insight and knowledge can be obtained from translating and transforming digitally represented information.
	EK 3.1.1E Patterns can emerge when data is transformed using computational tools.

7. **Answer: A.** While most scientists are not legally compelled to share their data, the norm is for them to make their data available for peer review so that other scientists can recreate their results, thereby confirming their discovery.

Learning Objectives	Essential Knowledge
LO 3.1.2 Collaborate when processing information to gain insight and knowledge.	EK 3.1.2A Collaboration is an important part of solving data-driven problems.

8. **Answer: C.** I and III accurately reflect the type of metadata that can be included in each of these file types, while II reflects the actual data in the file type.

Learning Objectives	Essential Knowledge
LO 3.2.1 Extract information from data to discover and explain connections and trends.	LO 3.2.1H Metadata can be descriptive data about an image, a webpage, or other complex object.

9. **Answer: D**. Information alchemy is a growing field that studies the methodologies of turning data and information into knowledge and eventually wisdom.

Learning Objectives	Essential Knowledge
LO 3.1.3 Explain the insight and knowledge gained from digitally processed data by using appropriate visualizations, notations, and precise language.	**EK 3.1.3D** Transforming information can be effective in communicating knowledge gained from data.

10. **Answer: B.** All of the selections are challenges faced by users of large data sets. Statement IV is false, as having more data sets available is not correlated to the techniques used to make calculations.

Learning Objectives	Essential Knowledge
LO 3.2.1 Extract information from data to discover and explain connections and trends.	**EK 3.2.1A** Large data sets provide opportunities and challenges for extracting information and knowledge.

4

Big Idea 4: Algorithms

Overview

Algorithms are used to develop and express solutions to computational problems.

Algorithms are being created, reused, analyzed, and improved on every day, and working with them is one of the most fundamental aspects of computing. You use algorithms throughout the AP® Computer Science Principles course as you develop ways to computationally solve problems. On the AP® Exam, you will be asked to evaluate algorithms to determine if they are correct, determine output, and identify specific techniques. Big Idea 4 is also assessed in the Create Performance Task.

Learning Objectives and Essential Knowledge Statements

LEARNING OBJECTIVES	ESSENTIAL KNOWLEDGE
LO. 4.1.1 Develop an algorithm for implementation in a program.	**EK 4.1.1A** Sequencing, selection, and iteration are building blocks of algorithms.
	EK 4.1.1B Sequencing is the application of each step of an algorithm in the order in which the statements are given.

LEARNING OBJECTIVES	ESSENTIAL KNOWLEDGE
LO. 4.1.1 (cont'd) Develop an algorithm for implementation in a program.	**EK 4.1.1C** Selection uses a Boolean condition to determine which of two parts of an algorithm is used.
	EK 4.1.1D Iteration is the repetition of part of an algorithm until a condition is met or for a specified number of times.
	EK 4.1.1E Algorithms can be combined to make new algorithms.
	EK 4.1.1F Using existing correct algorithms as building blocks for constructing a new algorithm helps ensure the new algorithm is correct.
	EK 4.1.1G Knowledge of standard algorithms can help in constructing new algorithms.
	EK 4.1.1H Different algorithms can be developed to solve the same problem.
	EK 4.1.1I Developing a new algorithm to solve a problem can yield insight into the problem.
LO 4.1.2 Express an algorithm in a language.	**EK 4.1.2A** Languages for algorithms include natural language, pseudocode, and visual and textual programming languages.
	EK 4.1.2B Natural language and pseudocode describe algorithms so that humans can understand them.
	EK 4.1.2C Algorithms described in programming languages can be executed on a computer.
	EK 4.1.2D Different languages are better suited for expressing different algorithms.

LEARNING OBJECTIVES	ESSENTIAL KNOWLEDGE
LO 4.1.2 (cont'd) Express an algorithm in a language.	**EK 4.1.2E** Some programming languages are designed for specific domains and are better for expressing algorithms in those domains. **EK 4.1.2F** The language used to express an algorithm can affect characteristics such as clarity or readability but not whether an algorithmic solution exists. **EK 4.1.2G** Every algorithm can be constructed using only sequencing, selection, and iteration. **EK 4.1.2H** Nearly all programming languages are equivalent in terms of being able to express any algorithm. **EK 4.1.2I** Clarity and readability are important considerations when expressing an algorithm in a language.
LO 4.2.1 Explain the difference between algorithms that run in a reasonable time and those that do not run in a reasonable time. EXCLUSION STATEMENT (for LO 4.2.1): Any discussion of nondeterministic polynomial (NP) is beyond the scope of this course and the AP® Exam.	**EK 4.2.1A** Many problems can be solved in a reasonable time. **EK 4.2.1B** Reasonable time means that the number of steps the algorithm takes is less than or equal to a polynomial function (constant, linear, square, cube, etc.) of the size of the input. EXCLUSION STATEMENT (for EK 4.2.1B) Using nonpolynomial functions to describe relationships between the number of steps required by an algorithm and the input size is beyond the scope of this course and the AP® Exam. **EK 4.2.1C** Some problems cannot be solved in a reasonable time, even for small inputs.

LEARNING OBJECTIVES	ESSENTIAL KNOWLEDGE
LO 4.2.1 (cont'd) Explain the difference between algorithms that run in a reasonable time and those that do not run in a reasonable time. EXCLUSION STATEMENT (for LO 4.2.1): Any discussion of nondeterministic polynomial (NP) is beyond the scope of this course and the AP® Exam.	**EK 4.2.1D** Some problems can be solved but not in a reasonable time. In these cases, heuristic approaches may be helpful to find solutions in reasonable time.
LO 4.2.2 Explain the difference between solvable and unsolvable problems in computer science. EXCLUSION STATEMENT (for LO 4.2.2): Determining whether a given problem is solvable or unsolvable is beyond the scope of this course and the AP® Exam.	**EK 4.2.2A** A heuristic is a technique that may allow us to find an approximate solution when typical methods fail to find an exact solution. **EK 4.2.2B** Heuristics may be helpful for finding an approximate solution more quickly when exact methods are too slow. EXCLUSION STATEMENT (for EK 4.2.2B) Specific heuristic solutions are beyond the scope of this course and the AP® Exam. **EK 4.2.2C** Some optimization problems such as "find the best" or "find the smallest" cannot be solved in a reasonable time but approximations to the optimal solution can. **EK 4.2.2D** Some problems cannot be solved using any algorithm.
LO 4.2.3 Explain the existence of undecidable problems in computer science.	**EK 4.2.3A** An undecidable problem may have instances that have an algorithmic solution, but there is no algorithmic solution that solves all instances of the problem. **EK 4.2.3B** A decidable problem is one in which an algorithm can be constructed to answer "yes" or "no" for all inputs (e.g., "is the number even?").

LEARNING OBJECTIVES	ESSENTIAL KNOWLEDGE
LO 4.2.3 (cont'd) Explain the existence of undecidable problems in computer science.	**EK 4.2.3C** An undecidable program is one in which no algorithm can be constructed that always leads to a correct yes-or-no answer. EXCLUSION STATEMENT (for EK 4.2.3C) Determining whether a given problem is undecidable is beyond the scope of this course and the AP® Exam.
LO 4.2.4 Evaluate algorithms analytically and empirically for efficiency, correctness, and clarity.	**EK 4.2.4A** Determining an algorithm's efficiency is done by reasoning formally or mathematically about the algorithm. **EK 4.2.4B** Empirical analysis of an algorithm is done by implementing the algorithm and running it on different inputs. **EK 4.2.4C** The correctness of an algorithm is determined by reasoning formally or mathematically about the algorithm, not by testing an implementation of the algorithm. EXCLUSION STATEMENT (for EK 4.2.4C) Formally proving program correctness is beyond the scope of this course and the AP® Exam. **EK 4.2.4D** Different correct algorithms for the same problem can have different efficiencies. **EK 4.2.4E** Sometimes, more efficient algorithms are more complex. **EK 4.2.4F** Finding an efficient algorithm for a problem can help solve larger instances of the problem.

LEARNING OBJECTIVES	ESSENTIAL KNOWLEDGE
LO 4.2.4 (cont'd) Evaluate algorithms analytically and empirically for efficiency, correctness, and clarity.	**EK 4.2.4G** Efficiency includes both execution time and memory usage. **EXCLUSION STATEMENT (for EK 4.2.4G)** Formal analysis of algorithms (Big-O) and formal reasoning using mathematical formulas are beyond the scope of this course and the AP® Exam. **EK 4.2.4H** Linear search can be used when searching for an item in any list; binary search can be used only when the list is sorted.

Practice Questions

1. A car repair chain is creating a new program to offer discounts and incentives to its customers through a series of rewards memberships. To qualify as a Silver Rewards member, a customer must visit the chain at least three times a year and spend at least $150 (United States dollars) annually. To qualify as a Gold Rewards member, a customer must visit the chain at least three times a year and spend at least $200 (United States dollars) annually. To qualify as a Platinum Rewards member, a customer must visit the chain at least three times a year and spend at least $500 (United States dollars) annually. They have a list which includes:
   - Customer names
   - Customer contact information
   - Number of customer visits in the last year
   - Total dollar amount spent in the last year

   Which algorithm, if any, can the chain use to identify members from a list of all customers?

   Algorithm I: Filter the data by creating a new list, ListOne of only customers that have spent $150 or more in the last year. Create a new list, Platinum. If a customer on ListOne has spent $500 or more in the last year, add the customer to Platinum and remove the customer from ListOne. Create a new list, Gold. If a customer on ListOne has spent $200 or more in the last year, add the customer to Gold and remove the customer from ListOne. Filter ListOne by creating a new list, Silver, of only customers that have visited three or more times in the last year.

   Algorithm II: Filter the data by creating a new list, ListOne, of only customers that have visited three times or more in the last year and have spent more than $150 in the last year. Create a new list, Platinum. If a customer on ListOne has spent $500 or more in the last year, add the customer to Platinum and remove the customer from ListOne. Create a new list, Gold. If a customer on ListOne has spent $200 or more in the last year, add the customer to Gold and remove the customer from ListOne. All remaining customers on ListOne are Silver members.

(A) I only
(B) II only
(C) Both I and II
(D) Neither I nor II

2. The following code segment finds the sum of all numbers, num, in list numList:

```
sum ← 0
FOR EACH num IN numList
{
    sum ← sum + n
}
```

What code segment will find the product of all numbers, num, in list numList?

(A) product← 1
```
        FOR EACH num IN numList
        {
            product← product + num
        }
```

(B) product← 1
```
        FOR EACH num IN numList
        {
            product← product * num
        }
```

(C) REPEAT UNTIL (LENGTH(numList)
```
        {
            product← product * num
        }
```

(D) REPEAT LENGTH(numList) TIMES
```
        {
            product← product * num
        }
```

3. List myList contains integer values. Which of the following code segments will remove all negative values from myList?

Algorithm I:
```
i ← 1
REPEAT LENGTH (myList) TIMES
{
   IF(myList[i]<0)
   {
       REMOVE(myList,i)
   }
i ← i + 1
}
```

Algorithm II:
```
i ← LENGTH(myList)
REPEAT LENGTH (myList) TIMES
{
   IF(myList[i]<0)
   {
       REMOVE(myList,i)
   }
i ← i - 1
}
```

(A) I only
(B) II only
(C) I and II
(D) Neither I nor II.

4. Consider a program that attempts to store the sum of all elements in listA that are greater than the previous element.

```
Line 1:    i ← 1
Line 2:    sum ← 0
Line 3:    REPEAT UNTIL (i > LENGTH (listA))
           {
Line 4:        IF (listA [i] > listA[i - 1])
               {
Line 5:            sum ← sum + listA[i - 1]
               }
Line 6:    i ← i + 1
           }
```

Choose two corrections that must be made in order to make the code run as expected.

(A) Line 1: i ← 2
(B) Line 3: REPEAT UNTIL (i ≥ LENGTH (listA))
(C) Line 5: sum ← sum + listA[i]
(D) Line 5: sum ← sum + listA[i + 1]

5. The halting problem is a problem which decides whether or not a program will run forever. Sometimes, it is easy to determine whether or not a program will run forever. Computer Scientist Alan Turing proved that there is no algorithmic solution to the halting problem that works for every algorithm. What is the halting problem an example of?
    (A) An undecidable problem
    (B) Levels of abstractions
    (C) A logic gate
    (D) Moore's Law

6. The question below uses a simple programming language, with the following instructions.
    The following program displays whether a number, x, is even.

    ```
    IF ( x MOD 2 = 0)
    {
        DISPLAY ("EVEN")
    }
    IF ( NOT x MOD 2 = 0)
    {
        DISPLAY ("NOT EVEN")
    }
    ```

    Choose <u>two</u> things that are true about the above problem.

    (A) The program uses Boolean algebra.
    (B) The program demonstrates a binary search.
    (C) The program, for certain values of x, will display both "EVEN" and "NOT EVEN".
    (D) The program provides a definite answer to the question, "Is x even?"

7. How is the correctness of an algorithm determined?
    (A) Testing all boundary conditions.
    (B) Reasoning formally or mathematically about the algorithm.
    (C) Testing all possible inputs.
    (D) Applying the Turing Test.

8. A mobile application developer wants to create a wardrobe app. She wants her app to offer clothing suggestions for the next four days based on weather predictions. Of the following choices, which is the <u>least difficult</u> way to connect weather predictions to her app?

(A) Research meteorology, update her findings daily, and push out updates to her app overnight so as not to inconvenience the users.

(B) Learn about which weather models are most accurate for a given region, replicate the models in her code, and use the phone's location detection to assign a model to the user's phone.

(C) Obtain and work with the API from a trusted weather forecaster's website to use their predictions as parameters for the wardrobe suggestions.

(D) Hire a meteorologist to create a new, ground-breaking model for weather prediction which can be incorporated into the code.

9. A computer science workshop presenter wants to write an algorithm to pair up participants based on birthdays. First, she wants to create pairs of participants with the same birthdays. She will pair up any remaining participants by finding the person with the closest birthday. Which of the following algorithms will correctly find all pairs of participants with the same birthdays? Select <u>two</u> answers.

(A)
  i. Make a copy of the list, called "Copy".
  ii. Select the first person on "Copy".
  iii. Complete a linear search to find someone else with the same birthday.
  iv. If there is a pair:
    1. Save the pair to a third and final list called "Pairs".
    2. Remove both people from "Copy".
    3. Go back to step ii.

(B)
  i. Select the first person on the participant list.
  ii. Complete a linear search of the participant list to find someone else with the same birthday.
  iii. If there are more participants on the list, repeat steps i and ii.

(C)
  i. Make a copy of the list, and call it "Copy".
  ii. Sort "Copy" by birthday.
  iii. Save every two consecutive participants into a new list called "Pairs".

(D)
  i. Make a copy of the list, and call it "Copy".
  ii. Sort "Copy" by birthday.
  iii. Save every two consecutive participants into a new list called "Pairs".
  iv. Select the first person on the "Copy" list.
  v. Complete a binary search of the participant list to find someone else with the same birthday.
  vi. If there are more participants on the list, repeat steps i and ii.

10. A student notices that members of the community are throwing recycling materials into the trash. He decides to create a mobile application to allow users to photograph an item, and the app would return information to the user about whether or not the item is recyclable. As he creates his program, he realizes that recycling programs can be confusing due to different procedures in different communities. He also begins to see patterns in images that help him determine if the item can be recycled. What is one possible explanation for what the student has learned?

(A) Developing a new algorithm to solve a problem can yield insight into the problem.

(B) Natural language and pseudocode describe algorithms so that humans can understand them.

(C) The language used to express an algorithm can affect characteristics such as clarity or readability but not whether an algorithmic solution exists.

(D) Clarity and readability are important considerations when expressing an algorithm in a language.

Answers

1. **Answer: B**. Only Algorithm II sorts all data for customers that have visited three or more times per year for all three membership levels.

Learning Objectives	Essential Knowledge
LO. 4.1.1 Develop an algorithm for implementation in a program.	**EK 4.1.1A** Sequencing, selection, and iteration are building blocks of algorithms.
	EK 4.1.1B Sequencing is the application of each step of an algorithm in the order in which the statements are given.
LO 4.1.2 Express an algorithm in a language.	**EK 4.1.2A** Languages for algorithms include natural pseudocode, and visual and textual programming languages.
	EK 4.1.2B Natural language and pseudocode describe algorithms so that humans can understand them.
LO 5.5.1 Employ appropriate mathematical and logical concepts in programming.	**EK 5.5.1F** Compound expressions using *and, or,* and *not* are part of most programming languages.

2. **Answer: B**. The code is identical to the sum question, with one change, multiplication.

Learning Objectives	Essential Knowledge
LO 4.1.1 Develop an algorithm for implementation in a program.	**EK 4.1.1E** Algorithms can be combined to make new algorithms.
LO 4.1.2 Express an algorithm in a language.	**EK 4.1.2B** Natural language and pseudocode describe algorithms so that humans can understand them.
LO 5.5.1 Employ appropriate mathematical and logical concepts in programming.	**EK 5.5.1D** Mathematical expressions using arithmetic operators are part of most programming languages.

3. **Answer: B**. Algorithm I, when it removes items, shifts all values down one. Therefore, consecutive negative numbers will be missed, and there could be an error for values of *i* close to the size of the list. Algorithm II addresses this issue by working backward.

Learning Objectives	Essential Knowledge
LO. 4.1.1 Develop an algorithm for implementation in a program.	**4.1.1A** Sequencing, selection, and iteration are building blocks of algorithms.
LO 4.1.2 Express an algorithm in a language.	**EK 4.1.2A** Languages for algorithms include natural pseudocode, and visual and textual programming languages.
LO 5.3.1 Use abstraction to manage complexity in programs.	**EK 5.3.1K** Lists and list operations, such as add, remove, and search, are common in many programs.

4. **Answers: A, C**. If *i* does not start at 2, there will be no value at listA[*i* – 1]. Also, we must add the actual list item, not the one before it, as shown in Line 5.

Learning Objectives	Essential Knowledge
LO. 4.1.1 Develop an algorithm for implementation in a program.	**EK 4.1.1A** Sequencing, selection, and iteration are building blocks of algorithms.
LO 4.1.2 Express an algorithm in a language.	**EK 4.1.2B** Natural language and pseudocode describe algorithms so that humans can understand them.
LO. 5.1.2 Develop a correct program to solve problems.	**EK 5.1.2A** An iterative process of program development helps in developing a correct program to solve problems.
LO 5.3.1 Use abstraction to manage complexity in programs.	**EK 5.3.1K** Lists and list operations, such as add, remove, and search, are common in many programs.

5. **Answer: A**. There is no algorithm to give a yes-or-no solution for all instances of the problem.

Learning Objectives	Essential Knowledge
LO 4.2.3 Explain the existence of undecidable problems in computer science.	**EK 4.2.3A** An undecidable problem may have instances that have an algorithmic solution, but there is no algorithmic solution that solves all instances of the problem.

6. **Answers: A, D**. The program is using Boolean algebra and produces a definite yes-or-no type answer.

Learning Objectives	Essential Knowledge
LO. 4.1.1 Develop an algorithm for implementation in a program.	**EK 4.1.1A** Sequencing, selection, and iteration are building blocks of algorithms.
LO 4.2.3 Explain the existence of undecidable problems in computer science.	**EK 4.2.3B** A decidable problem is one in which an algorithm can be constructed to answer "yes" or "no" for all inputs (e.g., "is the number even?").

7. **Answer: B**. The correctness of an algorithm is determined by reasoning formally or mathematically about the algorithm.

Learning Objectives	Essential Knowledge
LO 4.2.4 Evaluate algorithms analytically and empirically for efficiency, correctness, and clarity.	**EK 4.2.4C** The correctness of an algorithm is determined by reasoning formally or mathematically about the algorithm.

8. **Answer: C.** Using code that is already correct will help ensure that her program's predictions are as accurate as possible.

Learning Objectives	Essential Knowledge
LO 4.1.1 Develop an algorithm for implementation in a program.	**EK 4.1.1F** Using existing correct algorithms as building blocks for constructing a new algorithm helps ensure the new algorithm is correct. **EK 4.1.1G** Knowledge of standard algorithms can help in constructing new algorithms.
LO 4.2.4 Evaluate algorithms analytically and empirically for efficiency, correctness, and clarity.	**EK 4.2.4D** Different correct algorithms for the same problem can have different efficiencies.

9. **Answers: B, D.** Choice B is simply a linear search. D, while not efficient, will yield the correct result.

Learning Objectives	Essential Knowledge
LO 4.1.1 Develop an algorithm for implementation in a program.	**EK 4.1.1G** Knowledge of standard algorithms can help in constructing new algorithms.
LO. 5.1.2 Develop a correct program to solve problems.	**EK 5.1.2I** A programmer's knowledge and skills affects how a program is developed and how it's used to solve a problem.

10. **Answer: A.** The scenario describes learning that may occur from trying to solve a problem.

Learning Objectives	Essential Knowledge
LO. 4.1.1 Develop an algorithm for implementation in a program.	**EK 4.1.1I** Developing a new algorithm to solve a problem can yield insight into the problem.

5

BIG IDEA 5: PROGRAMMING

OVERVIEW

Programming enables problem solving, human expression, and creation of knowledge.

Programs are used to solve problems or to express creativity. This course will introduce you to the concepts and techniques related to writing programs, developing software, and using software effectively. Using algorithms and the language of your choice, you will write your own program in the Create—Applications from Ideas Performance Task. On the AP® Exam, programs are written in either block or text form, as you will see in the Practice Review Questions in this chapter. To prepare for the programming assessment, make sure that you are familiar with the reference sheet (see Appendix). You do NOT need to memorize the reference, but you should certainly get some practice in using it.

LEARNING OBJECTIVES AND ESSENTIAL KNOWLEDGE STATEMENTS

LEARNING OBJECTIVES	ESSENTIAL KNOWLEDGE
LO. 5.1.1 Develop a program for creative expression, to satisfy personal curiosity, or to create new knowledge.	**EK 5.1.1A** Programs are developed and used in a variety of ways by a wide range of people depending on the goals of the programmer.

LEARNING OBJECTIVES	ESSENTIAL KNOWLEDGE
LO. 5.1.1 (cont'd) Develop a program for creative expression, to satisfy personal curiosity, or to create new knowledge.	**EK 5.1.1B** Programs developed for creative expression, to satisfy personal curiosity, or to create new knowledge may have visual, audible, or tactile inputs and outputs.
	EK 5.1.1C Programs developed for creative expression, to satisfy personal curiosity, or to create new knowledge may be developed with different standards or methods than programs developed for widespread distribution.
	EK 5.1.1D Additional desired outcomes may be realized independently of the original purpose of the program.
	EK 5.1.1E A computer program or the results of running a program may be rapidly shared with a large number of users and can have widespread impact on individuals, organizations, and society.
	EK 5.1.1F Advances in computing have generated and increased creativity in other fields.
LO 5.1.2 Develop a correct program to solve problems.	**EK 5.1.2A** An iterative process of program development helps in developing a correct program to solve problems.
	EK 5.1.2B Developing correct program components and then combining them helps in creating correct programs.
	EK 5.1.2C Incrementally adding tested program segments to correct working programs helps create large correct programs.

LEARNING OBJECTIVES	ESSENTIAL KNOWLEDGE
LO 5.1.2 (cont'd) Develop a correct program to solve problems.	**EK 5.1.2D** Program documentation helps programmers develop and maintain correct programs to efficiently solve problems.
	EK 5.1.2E Documentation about program components, such as code segments and procedures, helps in developing and maintaining programs.
	EK 5.1.2F Documentation helps in developing and maintaining programs when working individually or in collaborative programming environments.
	EK 5.1.2G Program development includes identifying programmer and user concerns that affect the solution to problems.
	EK 5.1.2H Consultation and communication with program users is an important aspect of program development to solve problems.
	EK 5.1.2I A programmer's knowledge and skill affects how a program is developed and how it is used to solve a problem.
	EK 5.1.2J A programmer designs, implements, tests, debugs, and maintains programs when solving problems.
LO 5.1.3 Collaborate to develop a program.	**EK 5.1.3A** Collaboration can decrease the size and complexity of tasks required of individual programmers.
	EK 5.1.3B Collaboration facilitates multiple perspectives in developing ideas for solving problems by programming.

LEARNING OBJECTIVES	ESSENTIAL KNOWLEDGE
LO 5.1.3 (cont'd) Collaborate to develop a program.	**EK 5.1.3C** Collaboration in the iterative development of a program requires different skills that developing a program alone. **EK 5.1.3D** Collaboration can make it easier to find and correct errors when developing programs. **EK 5.1.3E** Collaboration facilitates developing program components independently. **EK 5.1.3F** Effective communication between participants is required for successful collaboration when developing programs.
LO 5.2.1 Explain how programs implement algorithms.	**EK 5.2.1A** Algorithms are implemented using program instructions that are processed during program execution. **EK 5.2.1B** Program instructions are executed sequentially. **EK 5.2.1C** Program instructions may involve variables that are initialized and updated, read, and written. **EK 5.2.1D** An understanding of instruction processing and program execution is useful for programming. **EK 5.2.1E** Program execution automates processes. **EK 5.2.1F** Processes use memory, a central processing unit (CPU), and input and output. **EK 5.2.1G** A process may execute by itself or with other processes.

LEARNING OBJECTIVES	ESSENTIAL KNOWLEDGE
LO 5.2.1 (cont'd) Explain how programs implement algorithms.	**EK 5.2.1H** A process may execute on one or several CPUs.
	EK 5.2.1I Executable programs increase the scale of problems that can be addressed.
	EK 5.2.1J Simple algorithms can solve a large set of problems when automated.
	EK 5.2.1K Improvements in algorithms, hardware, and software increase the kinds of problems and the size of problems solvable by programming.
LO. 5.3.1 Use abstraction to manage complexity in programs.	**EK 5.3.1A** Procedures are reusable programming abstractions.
	EK 5.3.1B A procedure is a named grouping of programming instructions.
	EK 5.3.1C Procedures reduce the complexity of writing and maintaining programs.
	EK 5.3.1D Procedures have names and may have parameters and return values.
	EK 5.3.1E Parameterization can generalize a specific solution.
	EK 5.3.1F Parameters generalize a solution be allowing a procedure to be used instead of duplicated code.
	EK 5.3.1G Parameters provide different values as input to procedures when they are called in a program.
	EK 5.3.1H Data abstraction provides a means of separating behavior from implementation.

LEARNING OBJECTIVES	ESSENTIAL KNOWLEDGE
LO. 5.3.1 (cont'd) Use abstraction to manage complexity in programs.	**EK 5.3.1I** Strings and string operations, including concatenation and some form of substring, are common in many programs.
	EK 5.3.1J Integers and floating-point numbers are used in programs without requiring understanding of how they are implemented.
	EK 5.3.1K List and list operations, such as add, remove, and search, are common in many programs.
	EK 5.3.1L Using lists and procedures as abstractions in programming can result in programs that are easier to develop and maintain.
	EK 5.3.1M Application program interfaces (APIs) and libraries simplify complex programming tasks.
	EK 5.3.1N Documentation for an API/library is an important aspect of programming.
	EK 5.3.1O APIs connect software components, allowing them to communicate.
LO. 5.4.1 Evaluate the correctness of a program.	**EK 5.4.1A** Program style can affect the determination of program correctness.
	EK 5.4.1B Duplicated code can make it harder to reason about a program.
	EK 5.4.1C Meaningful names for variables and procedures help people better understand programs.
	EK 5.4.1D Longer code segments are harder to reason about than shorter code segments in a program.

LEARNING OBJECTIVES	ESSENTIAL KNOWLEDGE
LO. 5.4.1 (cont'd) Evaluate the correctness of a program.	**EK 5.4.1E** Locating and correcting errors in a program is called debugging the program.
	EK 5.4.1F Knowledge of what a program is supposed to do is required in order to find most program errors.
	EK 5.4.1G Examples of intended behavior on specific inputs help people understand what a program is supposed to do.
	EK 5.4.1H Visual displays (or different modalities) of program state can help in finding errors.
	EK 5.4.1I Programmers justify and explain a program's correctness.
	EK 5.4.1J Justification can include a written explanation about how a program meets its specifications.
	EK 5.4.1K Correctness of a program depends on correctness of program components, including code segments and procedures.
	EK 5.4.1L An explanation of a program helps people understand the functionality and purpose of it.
	EK 5.4.1M The functionality of a program is often described by how a user interacts with it.
	EK 5.4.1 N The functionality of a program is best described at a high level by what the program does, not at the lower level of how the program statements work to accomplish this.

LEARNING OBJECTIVES	ESSENTIAL KNOWLEDGE
LO 5.5.1 Employ appropriate mathematical and logical concepts in programming.	**EK 5.5.1A** Numbers and numerical concepts are fundamental to programming. **EK 5.5.1B** Integers may be constrained in the maximum and minimum values that can be represented in a program because of storage limitations. EXCLUSION STATEMENT (for EK 5.5.1B) Specific range limitations of all programming languages are beyond the scope of this course and the AP® Exam. **EK 5.5.1C** Real numbers are approximated by floating-point representations that do not necessarily have infinite precision. EXCLUSION STATEMENT (for EK 5.5.1C) Specific sets of values that cannot be exactly represented by floating-point numbers are beyond the scope of this course and the AP® Exam. **EK 5.5.1D** Mathematical expressions using arithmetic operators are part of most programming languages. **EK 5.5.1E** Logical concepts and Boolean algebra are fundamental to programming. **EK 5.4.1F** Compound expressions using *and, or,* and *not* are part of most programming languages. **EK 5.4.1G** Intuitive and formal reasoning about program components using Boolean concepts helps in developing correct programs. **EK 5.5.1H** Computational methods may use lists and collections to solve problems.

LEARNING OBJECTIVES	ESSENTIAL KNOWLEDGE
LO 5.5.1 (cont'd) Employ appropriate mathematical and logical concepts in programming.	**EK 5.5.1I** Lists and other collections can be treated as abstract data types (ADTs) in developing programs. **EK 5.5.1J** Basic operations on collections include adding elements, removing elements, iterating over all elements, and determining whether an element is in a collection.

Practice Questions

A number of the programming problems involve a robot in a grid of squares. The following are examples of these types of problems:

1. The robot below has an additional method, ROTATE_LEFT (), in which the robot rotates in place 90 degrees counter-clockwise (i.e., makes an in-place left turn).

   Consider a robot who would like to move in an "L" shape.

   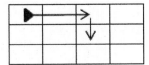

   Which of the following code segment will allow the robot to move in an L shape, assuming the path is clear:

   (A) MOVE_FORWARD ()
       MOVE_FORWARD ()
       ROTATE_LEFT ()
       ROTATE_LEFT ()
       ROTATE_LEFT ()
       MOVE_FORWARD ()

   (B) MOVE_FORWARD ()
       ROTATE_RIGHT ()
       MOVE_FORWARD ()
       MOVE_FORWARD ()

   (C) MOVE_FORWARD ()
       MOVE_FORWARD ()
       ROTATE_LEFT ()
       ROTATE_LEFT ()
       MOVE_FORWARD ()

   (D) MOVE_FORWARD ()
       MOVE_FORWARD ()
       ROTATE_LEFT ()
       ROTATE_LEFT ()
       MOVE_FORWARD ()

2. Consider the code segment below:

```
IF (CAN_MOVE(forward))
{
  MOVE_FORWARD()
}
  ROTATE_RIGHT ()
  ROTATE_RIGHT()
IF (NOT CAN_MOVE(right))
{
  MOVE_FORWARD ()
  ROTATE_RIGHT ()
  ROTATE_RIGHT()
}
```

For the following initial situation, what will be the final position and direction of the robot after the code is executed?

(A)

(B)

(C)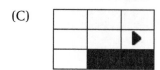

(D)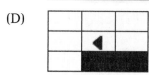

3. Consider the code segment below:

```
IF (CAN_MOVE(forward))
{
  MOVE_FORWARD ()
}
IF (NOT CAN_MOVE (forward))
{
  ROTATE_RIGHT()
  ROTATE_RIGHT()
}
```

For the following initial situation, what will be the final position and direction of the robot after the code is executed?

(A)

(B) ▢ ▶

(C) ◀ ▢

(D) ▶ ▢

4. Consider the code segment below:

```
REPEAT UNTIL (NOT CAN_MOVE(right))
{
  IF(CAN_MOVE (forward))
  {
    MOVE_FORWARD()
  }
  IF(NOT CAN_MOVE (forward))
  {
    ROTATE_RIGHT ()
    ROTATE_RIGHT ()
    MOVE_FORWARD()
  }
}
```

The code does not run as intended for the robot in the following scenario. Why not?

(A) The initial condition is not met, so the code in the REPEAT UNTIL loop is not executed.
(B) The robot backs up, then does not move.
(C) The program terminates when the robot attempts to move off the grid.
(D) There is an infinite loop.

5. Consider the code segment below:

```
REPEAT UNTIL (NOT CAN_MOVE(right))
{
  IF(CAN_MOVE (forward))
  {
    MOVE_FORWARD()
  }
  IF(NOT CAN_MOVE (forward))
  {
    ROTATE_RIGHT ()
    ROTATE_RIGHT ()
    MOVE_FORWARD()
  }
}
```

For the following initial situation, what will be the final position and direction of the robot after the code is executed?

(A)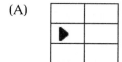

(B)

(C) The program terminates when the robot attempts to move off the grid.

(D) There is an infinite loop.

6. Consider the following code segment:

```
REPEAT UNTIL (CAN_MOVE (forward))
{
  ROTATE_RIGHT ( )
}
```

Which of the following are possible outcomes of the above code? Select two answers.

(A) The robot will move forward.
(B) The robot will return to its original position.
(C) The robot will be in a position in which it can move forward.
(D) The robot will get stuck in an infinite loop.

7. Consider the following scenario:

What will be the final location and direction of the robot after the following code segment is run?

```
REPEAT UNTIL (NOT CAN_MOVE (forward))
{
  IF (CAN_MOVE (right))
  {
     ROTATE_RIGHT ()
     MOVE_FORWARD ()
  }
  ELSE
  {
     MOVE_FORWARD ()
  }
}
```

(A)

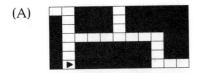

(B)

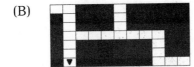

(C)

(D)

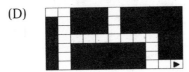

8. Consider the following incorrect code segment, meant to guide a robot through the maze below:

```
REPEAT UNTIL (NOT (CAN_MOVE (right) OR CAN_MOVE
(left) OR CAN_MOVE (forward) OR CAN_MOVE
(backward)))
{
  IF (CAN_MOVE(forward))
  {
    MOVE_FORWARD ()
  }
  ELSE
  {
    ROTATE_RIGHT ()
  }
}
```

In order to find out why the code is not working, the programmer views the robot at different points in the code. Immediately after which point will the robot not move as expected?

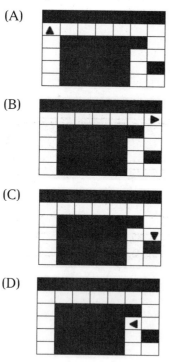

(A)

(B)

(C)

(D)

In addition to text-based code segments, there are also blocks-based code segments like the following, which can also be completed with the help of the Reference Sheet:

9. How many times will the following loop be executed?

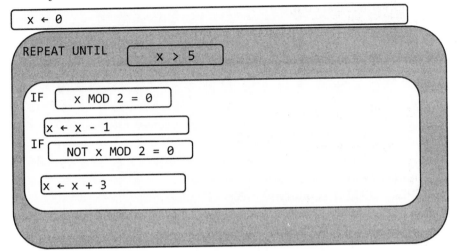

(A) The loop will not execute.
(B) 3
(C) 6
(D) There is an infinite loop.

10. Assuming that and *a* and *b* are integers, and *b* is less than zero, what can we assume is true after the following code is executed? Select <u>two</u> answers.

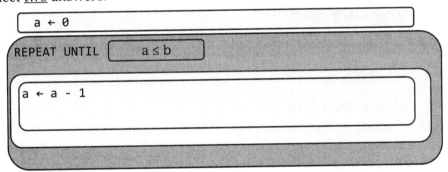

(A) a must be negative
(B) a may be zero
(C) a must be less than b
(D) a must equal b

Here is a variety of additional Programming Practice Problems:

11. Which of the following code segments from procedures will display "CS Principles" 5 times? Select <u>two</u> answers.

(A)
```
counter ← 0
REPEAT UNTIL (counter > 5)
{
  DISPLAY ("CS PRINCIPLES")
         counter ← counter + 1
}
```

(B)
```
REPEAT 5 TIMES
{
  DISPLAY ("CS PRINCIPLES")
       }
```

(C)
```
counter ← 1
REPEAT UNTIL (counter = 5)
{
  DISPLAY ("CS PRINCIPLES")
         counter ← counter + 1
}
```

(D)
```
counter ← 0
REPEAT UNTIL (counter = 100)
{
  DISPLAY ("CS PRINCIPLES")
       counter ← counter + 1
           IF (counter = 5)
     {
       RETURN counter
     }
}
```

12. The following procedure takes two lists, listA and listB, and adds the values of the elements together and saves them in a third list, listC.

```
PROCEDURE addLists (listA, listB, listC)
  {
    FOR EACH item IN list
    {
    listC[item] ← listA[item] + listB[item]
    }
  }
```

If a user wants to double the values in singleList and save them to doubleList, what is the appropriate way to call the procedure?

(A) addLists (singleList, singleList, doubleList)
(B) addLists (singleList, doubleList)
(C) addLists (doubleList, singleList)
(D) addLists (singleList (2), doubleList)

13. The following incomplete code simulates a game. The roll (n) procedure returns the sum of number cubes (numbered 1 – 6).

```
total ← roll (2)
IF (total < 8)
{
   total ← roll (1) + total
}
IF (total MOD 4 = 0)
{
   total ← total / 4
}
```

What would the value of total be if the first time that roll (2) is executed in the above segment, the values on the number cubes were 5 and 6?

(A) 3
(B) 11
(C) 22
(D) It is impossible to make that determination, as roll (number) is executed more than once in the program.

14. Consider the procedures concatenate(word1, word2), which returns a new string, combining word1 and word2, and substring(word1, n1, n2), which returns all characters from word1 beginning at the n1th character of the word up to and including the n2th character.
For example, concatenate("quick", "sand") will return the string "quicksand". Also, substring("shuttle", 2, 4) will return the string "hut". After lines 1 – 3 are executed, what will line 4 display?

```
LINE 1:   firstWord ← "computer"
LINE 2:   secondWord ← "science"
LINE 3:   thirdWord ← concatenate(secondWord, firstWord)
LINE 4:   DISPLAY (substring(thirdWord, 5, 10))
```

(A) "utersc"
(B) "uters"
(C) "ncecom"
(D) "nceco"

15. Consider the procedure mystery (num):

```
PROCEDURE mystery (num)
{
  value ← 0
  IF (num > 10)
  {
   value ← value + num * 2
  }
  ELSE
  {
    value ← value - num * 2
  }
  IF (num < 12)
  {
   value ← value * 2
  }
  value ← value * 2
  RETURN (value)
}
```

What is returned by a call to mystery (11) ?

(A) 0
(B) 22
(C) 44
(D) 88

16. Consider the procedure mystery (num):

```
PROCEDURE mystery (num)
{
  value ← 0
  IF (num > 10)
  {
   value ← value + num * 2
  }
  ELSE
  {
    value ← value + num
  }
  IF (num < 12)
  {
   value ← value * 2
  }
  value ← value * 2
  RETURN value
}
```

What is returned by a call to mystery (8) ?
(A) 8
(B) 16
(C) 32
(D) 64

17. Which of the following code segments will display: 1 4 9 16 ?

```
I.  num ← 1
    REPEAT 4 TIMES
      {
        square ← num * num
        DISPLAY (square)
        num ← num + 1
      }

II. num ← 1
    adder ← 3
    REPEAT 4 TIMES
      {
        DISPLAY (num)
        num ← num + adder
        adder ← adder + 2
      }
```

(A) I only
(B) II only
(C) I and II
(D) Neither I nor II

18. Consider the procedure mystery (num1, num2). Assume that num1 and num2 are positive numbers.

```
PROCEDURE mystery (num1, num2)
{
  i ← 0
  counter ← 1
  REPEAT UNTIL (counter > num1)
  {
    IF (num1 MOD counter == 0)
      {
        IF (num2 MOD counter == 0)
        {
          i ← i + 1
        }
      }
    counter ← counter + 1
  }
  RETURN i
}
```

What does mystery (num1, num2) return?

(A) The number of digits between num1 and num2.
(B) The number of even digits between num1 and num2.
(C) The number of odd digits between num1 and num2.
(D) The number of digits by which both num1 and num2 are divisible.

19. Consider the following procedure:

```
PROCEDURE mystery (n)
{
    sum ← 0
    REPEAT UNTIL ( n = 0)
    {
        IF (n MOD 3 ≠ 0)
        {
            sum ← sum + n
        }
        n ← n - 1
    }
    RETURN (sum)
}
```

What does mystery (9) return?

(A) 9
(B) 18
(C) 26
(D) 27

20. Consider the following procedure:

```
PROCEDURE mystery (list)
{
    FOR EACH item IN list
    {
        IF (item = 'a' OR item = 'e' OR item = 'i' OR
        item ='o' OR item = 'u')
        DISPLAY (item)
    }
}
```

If myList contains the values ['b', 'i', 'n', 'a', 'r', 'y'], What does mystery (myList) display?

(A) binary
(B) bnry
(C) ia
(D) iay

21. A group of students with no coding experience decide to develop an anti-bullying mobile application. Which of the following will make their work easier? Select two answers.
(A) They may make use of other code, accessible through APIs.
(B) Blocks editors require little understanding of control structures.
(C) Working together, each individual's tasks are smaller.
(D) Programmers can save time by working alone, as all properly written code that has been adequately tested will work when combined with other working code.

22. Consider the following code segment:

```
count ← 0
index ← 0
REPEAT LENGTH (numList) TIMES
{
  IF (numList [index] > numList [1]
  {
    count ← count + 1
  }
  index ← index + 1
}
```

Determine the value of count if the values in numList are 1, 5, 6, 3, 3, 1.

(A) 1
(B) 2
(C) 3
(D) 4

23. Consider the following code segment:

```
count ← 0
index ← 2
REPEAT LENGTH (numList) - 1 TIMES
{
  IF (numList [index] > numList [index - 1]
  {
    count ← count + 1
  }
  index ← index + 1
}
```

Determine the value of count if the values in numList are 1, 5, 6, 3, 3, 1.

(A) 1
(B) 2
(C) 3
(D) 4

24. Consider the following procedure, meant to iterate through a list of test questions in random order, displaying then removing them:

```
PROCEDURE QUIZ_ME ()
{
  REPEAT UNTIL ( LENGTH (quiz) = 0)
  {
    index ← RANDOM(1, LENGTH (quiz))
  /* missing code */
  }
}
```

What should replace /* missing code */ ?

(A) `DISPLAY (quiz [index])`
      `REMOVE (quiz [index])`
(B) `REMOVE (quiz [index])`
      `DISPLAY (quiz [index])`
(C) Both A and B will work.
(D) Neither A nor B will work.

25. Which of the following is true of collaboration? Select <u>two</u> answers.
    (A) Collaboration keeps participants focused and sharing a similar mindset.
    (B) Collaboration requires a different skill set than coding alone.
    (C) Collaboration requires all parts be completed together.
    (D) Collaboration eases the debugging process.

26. From a procedure using a simple programming language, which of the following lines of code contains an error (assuming all values have been defined previously)?
    (A) `DISPLAY (LENGTH (list)`
    (B) `DISPLAY ("Hello!")`
    (C) `DISPLAY (list [item])`
    (D) `DISPLAY (a < b)`

Answers

1. **Answer: A.** Rotating left three times is the same thing as rotating right once.

Learning Objectives	Essential Knowledge
LO 5.5.1 Employ appropriate mathematical and logical concepts in programming.	**EK 5.5.1E** Logical concepts and Boolean algebra are fundamental to programming.

2. **Answer: B.** The first if statement is executed, then the ROTATE_RIGHT ()s, but the last if statement is not executed.

Learning Objectives	Essential Knowledge
LO 5.5.1 Employ appropriate mathematical and logical concepts in programming.	**EK 5.5.1E** Logical concepts and Boolean algebra are fundamental to programming.

3. **Answer: D.** Both if statements are executed.

Learning Objectives	Essential Knowledge
LO 5.5.1 Employ appropriate mathematical and logical concepts in programming.	**EK 5.5.1E** Logical concepts and Boolean algebra are fundamental to programming.

4. **Answer: A.** The initial condition is never met, and the robot does not enter the loop.

Learning Objectives	Essential Knowledge
LO 5.5.1 Employ appropriate mathematical and logical concepts in programming.	**EK 5.5.1E** Logical concepts and Boolean algebra are fundamental to programming.

5. **Answer: D.** The robot continues to turn around and move forward.

Learning Objectives	Essential Knowledge
LO 5.5.1 Employ appropriate mathematical and logical concepts in programming.	**EK 5.5.1E** Logical concepts and Boolean algebra are fundamental to programming.

6. **Answers: C, D.** Choice C will work if there is a free position for the robot to move to; otherwise, there will be an infinite loop, as in Choice D.

Learning Objectives	Essential Knowledge
LO 5.5.1 Employ appropriate mathematical and logical concepts in programming.	**EK 5.5.1E** Logical concepts and Boolean algebra are fundamental to programming.

7. **Answer: C.** After the loop iterates once, the initial condition is no longer met.

Learning Objectives	Essential Knowledge
LO 5.5.1 Employ appropriate mathematical and logical concepts in programming.	EK 5.5.1E Logical concepts and Boolean algebra are fundamental to programming.

8. **Answer: D.** While making only right turns, the robot will turn around instead of turning left.

Learning Objectives	Essential Knowledge
LO. 5.4.1 Evaluate the correctness of a program.	EK 5.4.1H Visual displays (or different modalities) of program state can help in finding errors.

9. **Answer: B.** After running though the loop 3 times, x is equal to 6.

Learning Objectives	Essential Knowledge
LO 5.5.1 Employ appropriate mathematical and logical concepts in programming.	EK 5.5.1E Logical concepts and Boolean algebra are fundamental to programming.

10. **Answer: A, D.** a and b must be equal and negative, since we know that b is negative and a continuously decreases by 1

Learning Objectives	Essential Knowledge
LO 5.5.1 Employ appropriate mathematical and logical concepts in programming.	EK 5.5.1E Logical concepts and Boolean algebra are fundamental to programming.

11. **Answers: B, D.** B is a loop that repeats 5 times. D exists the procedure when counter reaches 5.

Learning Objectives	Essential Knowledge
LO 5.5.1 Employ appropriate mathematical and logical concepts in programming.	EK 5.5.1E Logical concepts and Boolean algebra are fundamental to programming.

12. **Answer: A.** singleList should be sent in twice as a parameter.

Learning Objectives	Essential Knowledge
LO 2.2.2 Use multiple levels of abstraction to write programs.	EK 2.2.2A Software is developed using multiple levels of abstraction, such as constants, expressions, statements, procedures, and libraries. EK 2.2.2B Being aware of and using multiple levels of abstraction in developing programs helps to more effectively apply available resources and tools to solve problems.
LO 5.3.1 Use abstraction to manage complexity in programs.	EK 5.3.1E Parameterization can generalize a specific solution.

Learning Objectives	Essential Knowledge
LO 5.5.1 Employ appropriate mathematical and logical concepts in programming.	EK 5.5.1I Lists and other collections can be treated as abstract data types (ADTs) in developing programs. EK 5.5.1J Basic operations on collections include adding elements, removing elements, iterating over all elements, and determining whether an element is in a collection.

13. **Answer: B.** The sum is found. None of the IF conditions are true, so the code in the curly braces does not execute.

Learning Objectives	Essential Knowledge
LO. 5.3.1 Use abstraction to manage complexity in programs.	EK 5.3.1F Parameters generalize a solution be allowing a procedure to be used instead of duplicated code.

14. **Answer: C.** thirdWord is sciencecomputer, and the fifth through tenth characters are ncecom.

Learning Objectives	Essential Knowledge
LO. 5.3.1 Use abstraction to manage complexity in programs.	EK 5.3.1D Procedures have names and may have parameters and return values. EK 5.3.1I Strings and string operations, including concatenation and some form of substring, are common in many programs.

15. **Answer: D.** value is num, doubled three times in the code.

Learning Objectives	Essential Knowledge
LO. 5.3.1 Use abstraction to manage complexity in programs.	EK 5.3.1A Procedures are reusable programming abstractions. EK 5.3.1B A procedure is a named grouping of programming instructions. EK 5.3.1G Parameters provide different values as input to procedures when they are called in a program.

16. **Answer: C.** value is increased by num, and then doubled twice.

Learning Objectives	Essential Knowledge
LO. 5.3.1 Use abstraction to manage complexity in programs.	EK 5.3.1A Procedures are reusable programming abstractions. EK 5.3.1B A procedure is a named grouping of programming instructions. EK 5.3.1G Parameters provide different values as input to procedures when they are called in a program. EK 5.3.1K List and list operations, such as add, remove, and search, are common in many programs.

17. **Answer: B**. I never changes the value of num.

Learning Objectives	Essential Knowledge
LO 5.5.1 Employ appropriate mathematical and logical concepts in programming.	**EK 5.5.1D** Mathematical expressions using arithmetic operators are part of most programming languages.
	EK 5.5.1E Logical concepts and Boolean algebra are fundamental to programming.

18. **Answer: D**. The procedure tests to see if num1 is divisible by counter, and if it is, checks the same for num2.

Learning Objectives	Essential Knowledge
LO. 5.3.1 Use abstraction to manage complexity in programs.	**EK 5.3.1A** Procedures are reusable programming abstractions.
	EK 5.3.1B A procedure is a named grouping of programming instructions.
	EK 5.3.1G Parameters provide different values as input to procedures when they are called in a program.

19. **Answer: D**. The code adds all values between 1 and 9 that are not divisible by 3.

Learning Objectives	Essential Knowledge
LO. 5.3.1 Use abstraction to manage complexity in programs.	**EK 5.3.1A** Procedures are reusable programming abstractions.
	EK 5.3.1B A procedure is a named grouping of programming instructions.
	EK 5.3.1G Parameters provide different values as input to procedures when they are called in a program.

20. **Answer: C**. The code prints out all vowels in the list.

Learning Objectives	Essential Knowledge
LO. 5.3.1 Use abstraction to manage complexity in programs.	**EK 5.3.1A** Procedures are reusable programming abstractions.
	EK 5.3.1B A procedure is a named grouping of programming instructions.
	EK 5.3.1G Parameters provide different values as input to procedures when they are called in a program.
	EK 5.3.1K List and list operations, such as add, remove, and search, are common in many programs.

21. **Answers: A, C**. APIs simply tasks, and collaboration decreases the size and complexity of tasks.

Learning Objectives	Essential Knowledge
LO. 5.3.1 Use abstraction to manage complexity in programs.	**EK 5.3.1M** Application program interfaces (APIs) and libraries simplify complex programming tasks.

22. **Answer: D**. There are 4 numbers greater than the first value in the list.

Learning Objectives	Essential Knowledge
LO. 5.3.1 Use abstraction to manage complexity in programs.	EK 5.3.1K List and list operations, such as add, remove, and search, are common in many programs.

23. **Answer: B**. There are two values greater than the preceding values in the list.

Learning Objectives	Essential Knowledge
LO. 5.3.1 Use abstraction to manage complexity in programs.	EK 5.3.1K List and list operations, such as add, remove, and search, are common in many programs.

24. **Answer: A**. The value must be displayed before it is removed.

Learning Objectives	Essential Knowledge
LO 5.5.1 Employ appropriate mathematical and logical concepts in programming.	EK 5.5.1J Basic operations on collections include adding elements, removing elements, iterating over all elements, and determining whether an element is in a collection.

25. **Answers: B, D**. Collaborating together is different from working alone, and makes finding errors easier.

Learning Objectives	Essential Knowledge
LO 5.1.3 Collaborate to develop a program.	EK 5.1.3B Collaboration facilitates multiple perspectives in developing ideas for solving problems by programming.
	EK 5.1.3C Collaboration in the iterative development of a program requires different skills that developing a program alone.
	EK 5.1.3D Collaboration can make it easier to find and correct errors when developing programs.
	EK 5.1.3E Collaboration facilitates developing program components independently.

26. **Answer: A**. There should be an additional closing parenthesis.

Learning Objectives	Essential Knowledge
LO. 5.1.1 Develop a program for creative expression, to satisfy personal curiosity, or to create new knowledge.	EK 5.1.1A Programs are developed and used in a variety of ways by a wide range of people depending on the goals of the programmer.
	EK 5.1.1B Programs developed for creative expression, to satisfy personal curiosity, or to create new knowledge may have visual, audible, or tactile inputs and outputs.

6

Big Idea 6:
The Internet

Overview

The Internet pervades modern computing.

The Internet is a collection of networks and devices all around the world. You will learn how the Internet works, as well as how and why the systems that it is built on work. You will learn about how it is changing with growth, and how its systems are scalable. You will learn about the positive and negative impacts of the use of the Internet, as well as cyber safety concerns. On the AP® Exam, you will be asked about characteristics of the Internet and how it works, the systems that are built on the Internet, and cybersecurity.

Learning Objectives and Essential Knowledge Statements

LEARNING OBJECTIVES	ESSENTIAL KNOWLEDGE
LO 6.1.1 Explain the abstractions in the Internet and how the Internet functions. EXCLUSION STATEMENT (for LO 6.1.1): Specific devices used to implement the abstractions in the Internet are beyond the scope of this course and the AP exam.	**EK 6.1.1A** The Internet connects devices and networks all over the world. **EK 6.1.1B** An end-to-end architecture facilitates connecting new devices and networks on the Internet.

LEARNING OBJECTIVES	ESSENTIAL KNOWLEDGE
LO 6.1.1 (cont'd) Explain the abstractions in the Internet and how the Internet functions. EXCLUSION STATEMENT (for LO 6.1.1): Specific devices used to implement the abstractions in the Internet are beyond the scope of this course and the AP exam.	**EK 6.1.1C** Devices and networks that make up the Internet are connected and communicate using addresses and protocols. **EK 6.1.1D** The Internet and the systems built on it facilitate collaboration. **EK 6.1.1E** Connecting new devices to the Internet is enabled by assignment of an Internet protocol (IP) address. **EK 6.1.1F** The Internet is built on evolving standards, including those for addresses and names. EXCLUSION STATEMENT (for EK 6.1.1F): Specific details of any particular standard for addresses are beyond the scope of this course and the AP® Exam. **EK 6.1.1G** The domain name system (DNS) translates domain names to IP addresses. **EK 6.1.1H** The number of devices that could use an IP address has grown so fast that a new protocol (IPv6) has been established to handle routing of many more devices. **EK 6.1.1I** Standards such as hypertext transfer protocol (HTTP), IP, and simple mail transfer protocol (SMTP) are developed and overseen by the Internet Engineering Task Force (IETF).
LO 6.2.1 Explain characteristics of the Internet and the systems built on it.	**EK 6.2.1A** The Internet and the systems built on it are hierarchical and redundant. **EK 6.2.1B** The domain name syntax is hierarchical.

LEARNING OBJECTIVES	ESSENTIAL KNOWLEDGE
LO 6.2.1 (cont'd) Explain characteristics of the Internet and the systems built on it.	**EK 6.2.1C** IP addresses are hierarchical. **EK 6.2.1D** Routing on the Internet is fault tolerant and redundant.
LO 6.2.2 Explain how the characteristics of the Internet influence the systems built on it.	**EK 6.2.2A** Hierarchy and redundancy help systems scale. **EK 6.2.2B** The redundancy of routing (i.e., more than one way to route data) between two points on the Internet increases the reliability of the Internet and helps it scale to more devices and more people. **EK 6.2.2C** Hierarchy in the DNS helps that system scale. **EK 6.2.2D** Interfaces and protocols enable widespread use of the Internet **EK 6.2.2E** Open standards fuel the growth of the Internet. **EK 6.2.2F** The Internet is a packet-switched system through which digital data is sent by breaking the data into blocks of bits called packets, which contain both the data being transmitted and control information for routing the data. EXCLUSION STATEMENT (for EK 6.2.2F): Specific details of any particular packet-switching system are beyond the scope of this course and the AP® Exam. **EK 6.2.2G** Standards for packets and routing included transmission control protocol/Internet protocol (TCP/IP). EXCLUSION STATEMENT (for EK 6.2.2G): Specific technical details of how TCP/IP works are beyond the scope of this course and the AP® exam.

LEARNING OBJECTIVES	ESSENTIAL KNOWLEDGE
LO 6.2.2 (cont'd) Explain how the characteristics of the Internet influence the systems built on it.	**EK 6.2.2H** Standards for sharing information and communicating between browsers and servers on the Web include HTTP and secure sockets layer/transport layer security (SSL/TLS). EXCLUSION STATEMENT (for EK 6.2.2H): Understanding the technical aspects of how SSL/TLS works is beyond the scope of this course and the AP® exam. **EK 6.2.2I** The size and speed of systems affect their use. **EK 6.2.2J** The bandwidth of a system is a measure of bit rate – the amount of data (measured in bits) that can be sent in a fixed amount of time. **EK 6.2.2K** The latency of a system is the time elapsed between the transmission and the receipt of a request.
LO 6.3.1 Identify existing cybersecurity concerns and potential options to address these issues with the Internet and the systems built on it.	**EK 6.3.1A** The trust model of the Internet involves trade-offs. **EK 6.3.1B** The DNS was not designed to be completely secure. **EK 6.3.1C** Implementing cybersecurity has software, hardware, and human components. **EK 6.3.1D** Cyberwarfare and cybercrime have widespread and potentially devastating effects. **EK 6.3.1E** Distributed denial-of-service attacks (DDoS) compromise a target by flooding it with requests from multiple systems. **EK 6.3.1F** Phishing, viruses, and other attacks have human and software components.

LEARNING OBJECTIVES	ESSENTIAL KNOWLEDGE
LO 6.3.1 (cont'd) Identify existing cybersecurity concerns and potential options to address these issues with the Internet and the systems built on it.	**EK 6.3.1G** Antivirus software and firewalls can help prevent unauthorized access to private data. **EK 6.3.1H** Cryptography is essential to many models of cybersecurity. **EK 6.3.1I** Cryptography has a mathematical foundation. EXCLUSION STATEMENT (for EK 6.3.1I): Specific mathematical functions used in cryptography are beyond the scope of this course and the AP® Exam. **EK 6.3.1J** Open standards help ensure cryptography is secure. **EK 6.3.1K** Symmetric encryption is a method of encryption involving one key for encryption and decryption. EXCLUSION STATEMENT (for EK 6.3.1K): The methods used in encryption are beyond the scope of this course and the AP® Exam. **EK 6.3.1L** Public key encryption, which is not symmetric, is an encryption method that is widely used because of the functionality it provides. EXCLUSION STATEMENT (for EK 6.3.1L): The mathematical methods used in public key cryptography are beyond the scope of this course and the AP® Exam. **EK 6.3.1M** Certificate authorities (CAs) issue digital certificates that validate the ownership and encrypted keys used in secured communications and are based on a trust model. EXCLUSION STATEMENT (for EK 6.3.1M): The technical details of the process CAs follow are beyond the scope of this course and the AP® exam.

Practice Questions

1. As technology has improved and gotten more cost-effective more people have been able to access the Internet. With this influx of users has come the need to increase the network's capacity for the growing amounts of data that can travel through it. Which of the following terms below defines that measurement?
   (A) baud rate
   (B) bandwidth
   (C) latency
   (D) broadband

2. Your friend Simon told you that he was called into the school office and accused of accessing an inappropriate web page on a school computer. He knows you understand how computers work and he asks if you can think of any way he can prove his innocence. Which of the following is the ***best*** indicator of Simon's innocence? (All actions are taken with the permission of the school.)
   (A) You review the browser history and cache for Simon's user name. The web page is not listed in either the browser history or the cache.
   (B) The web page in question is designed to store a cookie on the client computer. Upon looking for the cookie you find that it does not exist on the school's computer.
   (C) You ask to review the schools DNS server logs which tracks the requests of all users. The school's DNS server was not used to access the IP address of the server that houses the inappropriate page.
   (D) You realize that the inappropriate page has an advertising frame that logs the visiting computers digital fingerprint on the advertiser's server. Upon investigation, you find that the advertiser's server does not contain the fingerprint for the school computer.

3. An online hacktivist group calling themselves Relevance has targeted an international distribution company website citing unfair practices when charging shipping rates. Relevance members have created bot programs that will continually send information requests to the company's servers during prime shopping times. These requests will come in from servers spread across the globe. The actions taken by Relevance are an example of what kind of cyber-attack?
   (A) socially engineered trojan
   (B) distributed denial of service
   (C) network traveling worm
   (D) advanced persistent threat

4. Look at the URL below. What does the highlighted portion most likely indicate?

    https://www.widgets.com/catalogs/fall/circular.aspx

    (A) the website being visited has been specified as a sales website as indicated by the "s" in the URL
    (B) the website has been certified to be free of ads and possible socially engineered trojans
    (C) the website is a secured website and can only be accessed by using a user account and password
    (D) a certificate authority has verified that the encryption keys used by the site owners are valid

5. Two students working on a project together don't want any of their classmates to be able to read their notes. In the course of their research, they come across the concept of a Caesar Cipher. In a Caesar Cipher letters are shifted a certain number of spaces down the alphabet. For example, if "c" represents "a", this would indicate a shift of two. The team's notes look like chaos to anyone who finds them, but can be decoded perfectly by reversing the shift. A Caesar Cipher is an example of which kind of encryption?
    (A) private key encryption
    (B) symmetric encryption
    (C) public key encryption
    (D) asymmetric encryption

6. Taylor and Emma are working on a school project together over spring break. Taylor is on vacation with her family while Emma is still at home. Rather than work on separate slide shows while they are apart and merge them after vacation, they want to work together on one presentation. What is the most efficient way to accomplish this goal?
    (A) They can create a slide show presentation and email it back and forth making changes based on feedback in the body of the email.
    (B) They decide to use a screen capture program that will record videos of them working on the presentation. They can then post the videos to a video service so their partner can take notes and see what work has been done.
    (C) They decide to use a cloud computing service where they can house one presentation and make notes and corrections to that document.
    (D) They decide to divide the work entirely and have one develop the slide show while the other writes a research paper that accompanies it.

7. Ian is a new employee at the ABC Widget Corporation. On his second day in the job, he receives an email from what appears to be a valid company email account. Attached to the email is a file that is titled "New Employee Handbook". Ian opens the email and opens the file only to receive a message that the file cannot be opened. A few weeks later, the IT department discovers that the company has been a target of an advanced persistent threat (APT). An APT is an attack on a system where someone gains access to a system and stays there, undetected, for a long period of time. What are the most likely causes and results of the APT? Select <u>two</u> answers.

(A) Through a form of social engineering, Ian inadvertently released a virus into the company's network. The virus will replicate itself and seek out important company financial files. Once it locates the desired financial records, the virus will delete the records in an attempt to cause severe financial implications for ABC Widget.

(B) An outside hacker was able to piggy back into the company's network through a security glitch in the company's website. Ian's actions were irrelevant. The hacker was able to plant a worm in the network which will seek out the company's customer database and randomly remove information.

(C) By opening the e-mail Ian has allowed a hacktivist group to place a spyware program on the company server. The group is looking for evidence of environmental policy violations at the company's manufacturing plant. Over the course of a few weeks the spyware was able to locate company memos regarding environmental impacts and email them to local media.

(D) Through a method known as spear phishing, Ian unknowingly allowed a competing company to get into ABC's network and gain access to its proprietary files. The corporate spy has had several weeks to peruse the network, stealing company financial records and proprietary product design information.

8. Kendall has been asked to talk with a small group of new teachers and explain how the Internet works. Which of the following explanations best describes the framework/architecture on which the Internet is built?

   (A) A user is sitting at her computer surfing the Internet and wants to download a recipe from a site. She hits the download button to initiate the file transfer. The request is broken down into a series of smaller segments called packets that are sent through multiple routers until they are put back together at the web server which processes and answers the request. The process is then repeated the other way going back to the user.

   (B) A user is sitting at her home computer and wants to download some pictures for a school project. The user finds the picture she wants to download and clicks on it. A message is sent to the web server where it locates the desired picture. That picture is then broken into smaller components that are reassembled at each node along the network until the user finally receives the picture that she requested.

   (C) A user is shopping online and wants to make some purchases. As she clicks on each item the data for that item is stored in the cache on the local machine. Once all of the items selected are sent to the online shopping cart, the user's machine sends a batch file across the Internet routing system to the ecommerce site's server. The batch file is then broken down into its various components (purchases, number of items, payment information, etc.) and routed appropriately.

   (D) A user wants to stream a live video feed from an online service. Once she selects the movie, the server takes the video and breaks it into ordered chunks of equal size. The server then sends the chunks in the correct order to the user who uses a video player to decode the chunks and play the video. When one chunk is done playing, the video server sends the next one.

9. With the proliferation of smart phones, laptops, tablets, and other personal computing devices, our "connectedness" continues to grow. However, with the number of manufacturers, ISPs, and providers of web-based content, actually getting on the web can sometimes feel like a daunting task. Which statement below best explains how the Internet can truly be a global entity?

   (A) The Internet is design with very strict standards that every hardware manufacturer, software developer, and ISP must adhere to in order for anyone to connect to the Internet.

   (B) The hardware, software, and connection standards are open and flexible enough to allow many different companies from all over the globe to develop Internet accessible products.

   (C) Internet protocols and standards vary within each country but specific, proprietary protocols and standards exist internationally to ensure that people from each country can connect to the web.

   (D) Internet protocols and standards are only suggested guidelines. The Internet operates on general guidelines for hardware, software, and communication. Until there are stricter controls, the Internet cannot be a true global meeting place.

10. Lisa is looking through papers left behind by some students after her class one day. She finds a scrap of paper with a strange letter series on it (see below). What word best describes what Lisa is looking at?

   Efn zj kyv kzdv wfi rcc xffu dve kf tfdv kf kyv rzu fw kyvzi tflekip. Kyv hlztb sifne wfo aldgvu fmvi kyv crqp ufx. Z rd ze cfmv nzky jfdvfev kyrk yrj jkfcve dp yvrik. Z ufe'k vmvi nrek kyvd kf xzmv zk srtb.

   (A) cryptographics
   (B) plaintext
   (C) ciphertext
   (D) cybertext

11. As part of your research on computer science careers you find many interesting job descriptions for which you would like more information. One description says the following: "Accessing data and computing power without being granted access but with permission of the system administrators …. their job is to identify and repair system vulnerabilities." Which of the following jobs is being described?
   (A) hacking
   (B) penetration testing
   (C) privilege escalation
   (D) black hatting

12. You are asked to look at a piece of a screen capture collected by a teacher. She is trying to figure out which computer in your classroom is listed here. She said the IT department told her she needed the IPv6 address so they could locate the machine in question. Which letter below identifies that address?

   (A) --   3C-A9-F4-19-58-E8
            Yes
            Yes
   (B) --   fe80::75f2:378c:f850:b679%16(Preferred)
            192.168.1.6(Preferred)
            255.255.255.0
            Sunday, November 08, 2015 3:07:27 PM
            Monday, November 09, 2015 3:07:26 PM
            192.168.1.1
   (C) --   192.168.1.1
            373074420
   (D) --   00-01-00-01-DA-67-53-8F-D8-9D-67-CE-C8-FE

            192.168.1.1
            Enabled

Answers

1. **Answer: B**. Bandwidth is the measure of the *amount* of data that is transmitted (for example, 3 bits per second) through the network. Baud rate measures the *rate* at which signals are sent through a network (for example, once per second), not how much data is sent in that time.

Learning Objectives	Essential Knowledge
LO 6.2.2 Explain how the characteristics of the Internet influence the systems built on it.	**EK 6.2.2J** The bandwidth of a system is a measure of bit rate – the amount of data (measured in bits) that can be sent in a fixed amount of time.

2. **Answer: C**. While several of these answers could have been correct, the <u>best</u> indicator of Simon's innocence would be the DNS log. Browser histories, caches, and cookies can be deleted. In addition, cookies and ads can be blocked by software added to the browser and will therefore not perform their desired function. Because the DNS log is not accessible by the client machine and students cannot modify it, the DNS log is the best indicator of innocence.

Learning Objectives	Essential Knowledge
LO 6.3.1 Identify existing cybersecurity concerns and potential options to address these issues with the Internet and the systems built on it.	**EK 6.3.1A** The trust model of the Internet involves trade-offs.

3. **Answer: B**. A Distributed denial of service attack (DDoS) is designed specifically to overload a target's servers with information requests from multiple system. A network traveling worm is a type of computer virus that can hide itself in a network and steal various types of information. An advanced persistent threat can sometimes be called spear phishing. It usually comes as a trojan in an email. Once the email is open, the trojan/APT is released compromising an entire system. A socially engineered trojan usually comes from what appears to be a trusted website. These attacks tell a user that something is wrong with their computer and they need to download a file to fix it. When the file is downloaded, the virus is then in place.

Learning Objectives	Essential Knowledge
LO 6.3.1 Identify existing cybersecurity concerns and potential options to address these issues with the Internet and the systems built on it.	**EK 6.3.1E** Distributed denial-of-service attacks (DDoS) compromise a target by flooding it with requests from multiple systems.

4. **Answer: D**. The https protocol means that a certificate authority (CA) has issued a certificate validating that the owner of the site uses encrypted keys for communication to and from the site.

Learning Objectives	Essential Knowledge
LO 6.3.1 Identify existing cybersecurity concerns and potential options to address these issues with the Internet and the systems built on it.	**EK 6.3.1M** Certificate authorities (CAs) issue digital certificates that validate the ownership and encrypted keys used in secured communications and are based on a trust model. EXCLUSION STATEMENT: The technical details of the process CAs follow are beyond the scope of this course and the AP® exam.

5. **Answer: B**. A Caesar Cipher is an example of symmetric encryption. Only one key exists for decoding the message (the number of letters shifted) and both parties to the encryption are aware of the shift.

Learning Objectives	Essential Knowledge
LO 6.3.1 Identify existing cybersecurity concerns and potential options to address these issues with the Internet and the systems built on it.	**EK 6.3.1K** Symmetric encryption is a method of encryption involving one key for encryption and decryption. EXCLUSION STATEMENT: The methods used in encryption are beyond the scope of this course and the AP® Exam.

6. **Answer: C**. A cloud computing service will allow the girls to work in real time on the same document making immediate changes that both can see and comment on. While the other suggestions are all valid options, none of them are as efficient as cloud computing.

Learning Objectives	Essential Knowledge
LO 6.1.1 Explain the abstractions in the Internet and how the Internet functions. EXCLUSION STATEMENT: Specific devices used to implement the abstractions in the Internet are beyond the scope of this course and the AP® Exam.	**EK 6.1.1D** The Internet and the systems built on it facilitate collaboration.

7. **Answers: C, D**. An advanced persistent threat (APT) is a network attack where the intent is to steal data and other information rather than destroying it.

Learning Objectives	Essential Knowledge
LO 6.3.1 Identify existing cybersecurity concerns and potential options to address these issues with the Internet and the systems built on it.	**EK 6.3.1C** Implementing cybersecurity has software, hardware, and human components. **EK 6.3.1D** Cyber warfare and cyber-crime have widespread and potentially devastating effect. **EK 6.3.1E** Distributed denial of service (DDoS) compromise a target by flooding it with requests from multiple systems. **EK 6.3.1F** Phishing, viruses, and other attacks have human and software components.

8. **Answer: A**. The Internet uses and end-to-end architecture in its design. All aspects of creating and reassembling data packets are done at each end of the network (i.e., user and server). Everything in between (routers, etc.) are strictly there for transmission purposes. They do nothing but move the packets from one place to another. While the other possible answers all have some aspects of validity, they are all missing this one key aspect of the Internet architecture.

Learning Objectives	Essential Knowledge
LO 6.1.1 Explain the abstractions in the Internet and how the Internet functions. EXCLUSION STATEMENT: Specific devices used to implement the abstractions in the Internet are beyond the scope of this course and the AP® Exam.	**EK 6.1.1B** An end-to-end architecture facilitates connecting new devices and networks on the Internet.

9. **Answer: B**. There are several international organizations that develop, monitor, and enforce a variety of standards and protocols for hardware, software, and connection methods for accessing the Internet. However, these standards and protocols are well-known and the information is open to anyone trying to design and/or develop tools for getting on the Internet.

Learning Objectives	Essential Knowledge
LO 6.2.2 Explain how the characteristics of the Internet influence the systems built on it.	**EK 6.2.2D** Interfaces and protocols enable widespread use of the Internet **EK 6.2.2E** Open standards fuel the growth of the Internet.

10. **Answer: C**. Ciphertext is a string of text that has been converted to a secure form using encryption.

Learning Objectives	Essential Knowledge
LO 6.3.1 Identify existing cybersecurity concerns and potential options to address these issues with the Internet and the systems built on it.	**EK 6.3.1H** Cryptography is essential to many models of cybersecurity.

11. **Answer: B**. Professional penetration testers are computer scientists who are paid to try to find ways into a supposedly secure system. They attempt to access the system with the full permission of the business owners and system administrators.

Learning Objectives	Essential Knowledge
LO 6.3.1 Identify existing cybersecurity concerns and potential options to address these issues with the internet and the systems built on it.	**EK 6.3.1A** The trust model of the Internet involves trade-offs.

12. **Answer: B**. IPv6 addresses do not use the decimal dotted system that IPv4 uses. The system has substantially more addresses and as such reads differently than a regular IP address.

Learning Objectives	Essential Knowledge
LO 6.1.1 Explain the abstractions in the Internet and how the Internet functions. EXCLUSION STATEMENT: Specific devices used to implement the abstractions in the Internet are beyond the scope of this course and the AP® Exam.	EK 6.1.1H The number of devices that could use an IP address has grown so fast that a new protocol (IPv6) has been established to handle the routing of many more devices.

7

BIG IDEA 7: GLOBAL IMPACT

OVERVIEW

Computing has global impact.

Computing has changed the way we communicate, collaborate, problem- solve, and do business. Advances in computing contribute to advances in many other fields as well, providing tools for new understanding, innovation and discovery. In this course, you will focus on impact in the through-course Performance Tasks, particularly in Explore—Impact of Computing Innovations. You will choose and investigate a computing innovation that has had significant beneficial and harmful effects on society, you will respond to prompts about that innovation, and create an artifact which illustrates, represents, or explains the computing innovation. You should pick a technology that you are very interested in, and that has known beneficial and harmful effects on society. The more that the innovation has impacted you directly, the more content you will have to reflect on, and the more inspired you will be in your artifact creation. To earn the maximum score, be sure you read the task guidelines carefully, and make certain your artifact is considered effective by the College Board's standards.

LEARNING OBJECTIVES AND ESSENTIAL KNOWLEDGE STATEMENTS

LEARNING OBJECTIVES	ESSENTIAL KNOWLEDGE
LO 7.1.1 Explain how computing innovations affect communication, interaction and cognition.	**EK 7.1.1A** Email, SMS, and chat have fostered new ways to communicate and collaborate.
	EK 7.1.1B Video conferencing and video chat have fostered new ways to communicate and collaborate.
	EK 7.1.1C Social media continues to evolve and fosters new ways to communicate.
	EXCLUSION STATEMENT (for EK 7.1.1C): Detailed knowledge of any social media site is beyond the scope of this course and the AP® Exam.
	EK 7.1.1D Cloud computing fosters new ways to communicate and collaborate.
	EK 7.1.1 E Widespread access to information facilitates the identification of problems, development of solutions, and dissemination of results.
	EK 7.1.1F Public data provides widespread access and enables solutions to identified problems.
	EK 7.1.1G Search trends are predictors.
	EK 7.1.1 H Social media, such as blogs and Twitter, have enhanced dissemination.
	EK 7.1.1I Global Positioning System (GPS) and related technologies have changed how humans travel, navigate, and find information related to geolocation.

LEARNING OBJECTIVES	ESSENTIAL KNOWLEDGE
LO 7.1.1 (cont'd) Explain how computing innovations affect communication, interaction and cognition.	**EK 7.1.1J** Sensor networks facilitate new ways of interacting with the environment and with physical systems. **EK 7.1.1K** Smart grids, smart buildings, and smart transportation are changing and facilitating human capabilities. **EK 7.1.1L** Computing contributes to many assistive technologies that enhance human capabilities. **EK 7.1.1M** The Internet and the Web have enhanced methods of and opportunities for communication and collaboration. **EK 7.1.1N** The Internet and the Web have changed many areas, including e-commerce, health care, access to information and entertainment, and online learning. **EK 7.1.1O** The Internet and the Web have impacted productivity, positively and negatively, in many areas.
LO 7.1.2 Explain how people participate in a problem-solving process that scales.	**EK 7.1.2A** Distributed solutions must scale to solve some problems. **EK 7.1.2B** Science has been impacted by using scale and "citizen science" to solve scientific problems using home computers in scientific research. **EK 7.1.2C** Human computation harnesses contributions from many humans to solve problems related to digital data and the Web. **EK 7.1.2D** Human capabilities are enhanced by digitally enabled collaboration.

LEARNING OBJECTIVES	ESSENTIAL KNOWLEDGE
LO 7.1.2 (cont'd) Explain how people participate in a problem-solving process that scales.	**EK 7.1.2E** Some online services use the contributions of many people to benefit both individuals and society. **EK 7.1.2F** Crowdsourcing offers new models for collaboration, such as connecting people with jobs and businesses with funding. **EK 7.1.2G** The move from desktop computers to a proliferation of always-on mobile computers is leading to new applications.
LO 7.2.1 Explain how computing has impacted innovations in other fields.	**EK 7.2.1A** Machine learning and data mining have enabled innovation in medicine, business, and science. **EK 7.2.1B** Scientific computing has enabled innovation in science and business. **EK 7.2.1C** Computing enables innovation by providing the ability to access and share information. **EK 7.2.1D** Open access and Creative Commons have enabled broad access to digital information. **EK 7.2.1E** Open and curated scientific databases have benefited scientific researchers. **EK 7.2.1F** Moore's Law has encouraged industries that use computers to effectively plan future research and development based on anticipated increases in computing power. **EK 7.2.1G** Advances in computing as an enabling technology have generated and increased the creativity in other fields.

LEARNING OBJECTIVES	ESSENTIAL KNOWLEDGE
LO 7.3.1 Analyze the beneficial and harmful effects of computing.	**EK 7.3.1A** Innovations enabled by computing raise legal and ethical concerns. **EK 7.3.1B** Commercial access to music and movie downloads and streaming raises legal and ethical concerns. **EK 7.3.1C** Access to digital content via peer-to-peer networks raises legal and ethical concerns. **EK 7.3.1D** Both authenticated and anonymous access to digital information raise legal and ethical concerns. **EK 7.3.1E** Commercial and governmental censorship of digital information raise legal and ethical concerns. **EK 7.3.1F** Open source and licensing of software and content raise legal and ethical concerns. **EK 7.3.1G** Privacy and security concerns arise in the development and use of computational systems and artifacts. **EK 7.3.1H** Aggregation of information, such as geolocation, cookies, and browsing history, raises privacy and security concerns. **EK 7.3.1I** Anonymity in online interactions can be enabled through the use of online anonymity software and proxy servers. **EK 7.3.1J** Technology enables the collection, use, and exploitation of information about, by, and for individuals, groups, and institutions.

LEARNING OBJECTIVES	ESSENTIAL KNOWLEDGE
LO 7.3.1 (cont'd) Analyze the beneficial and harmful effects of computing.	**EK 7.3.1K** People can have instant access to vast amounts of information online; accessing this information can enable the collection of both individual and aggregate data that can be used and collected.
	EK 7.3.1L Commercial and governmental curation of information may be exploited if privacy and other protections are ignored.
	EK 7.3.1M Targeted advertising is used to help individuals but it can be misused at both individual and aggregate levels.
	EK 7.3.1N Widespread access to digitized information raises questions about intellectual property.
	EK 7.3.1O Creation of digital audio, video, and textual content by combining existing content has been impacted by copyright concerns.
	EK 7.3.1P The Digital Millennium Copyright Act (DMCA) has been a benefit and a challenge in making copyrighted digital material widely available.
	EK 7.3.1Q Open source and free software have practical, business, and ethical impacts on widespread access to programs, libraries, and code.
LO 7.4.1 Explain the connections between computing and real-world contexts, including economic, social, and cultural contexts.	**EK 7.4.1A** The innovation and impact of social media and online access varies in different countries and in different socioeconomic groups.
	EK 7.4.1B Mobile, wireless, and networked computing have an impact on innovation throughout the world.

LEARNING OBJECTIVES	ESSENTIAL KNOWLEDGE
LO 7.4.1 (cont'd) Explain the connections between computing and real-world contexts, including economic, social, and cultural contexts.	**EK 7.4.1C** The global distribution of computing resources raises issues of equity, access, and power. **EK 7.4.1D** Groups and individuals are affected by the "digital divide" – differing access to computing and the Internet based on socioeconomic or geographic characteristics. **EK 7.4.1E** Networks and infrastructure are supported by both commercial and governmental initiatives.
LO 7.5.1 Access, manage, and attribute information using effective strategies.	**EK 7.5.1A** Online databases and libraries catalog and house secondary and some primary sources. **EK 7.5.1B** Advance search tools, Boolean logic, and key words can refine the search focus and/or limit search results based on a variety of factors (e.g., data, peer-review status, type of publication). **EK 7.5.1C** Plagiarism is a serious offense that occurs when a person presents another's ideas or words as his or her own. Plagiarism may be avoided by accurately acknowledging sources.
LO 7.5.2 Evaluate online and print sources for appropriateness and credibility.	**EK 7.5.2A** Determining the credibility of a source requires considering and evaluating the reputation and credentials of the author(s), publisher(s), site owner(s), and/or sponsor(s). **EK 7.5.2B** Information from a source is considered relevant when it supports an appropriate claim or the purpose of the investigation.

Practice Questions

1. The power of the Internet is not just for MMORPRGs or posting selfies. Many sites on the web allow users to connect and contribute to individuals, groups, and society as a whole in countless ways. Look through the list below and select the answer that is least likely to occur as a result of online collaboration.
   (A) Using a citizen science site, a medical team researching the molecular strain that is involved in the spreading of the AIDS virus was able to find a chemical key that could help them develop a drug that might stop the virus.
   (B) Using an online information database, a group of people who like to solve criminal cold cases was able to view police files regarding the infamous Jack the Ripper case, an old, unsolved crime. After many months of reviewing the files, the group was able to determine the real identity of Jack the Ripper.
   (C) Two men went on a ski trip in the Swiss Alps and became separated from their group during a snowstorm. A member of their team used social media to get phone numbers for the missing snowboarders. One of the men was contacted on his mobile phone and used his a mobile map application to send rescuers the longitude and latitude of his location.
   (D) A Twenty-two-month-old baby had been fighting infant leukemia since birth, and her family couldn't find a bone marrow donor to match her rare type. Her parents made an appeal on social media and more than 5,500 people around the world signed up. Eventually, a match was found in Australia.

2. Several scientists are taking advantage of the Internet as the users of it to enhance and expedite their scientific research. Scientists are enlisting the assistance of the users of the World Wide Web to help with research on topics such as hummingbird migration, whale shark migration, and the severity of earthquakes, just to name a few. Which of the following are NOT limitations to "citizen scientists" helping with scientific research? Select two answers.
   (A) If volunteers lack proper training in research and monitoring protocols, they are at risk of introducing bias into the data.
   (B) Scientific research should only be conducted by professional scientists who can collect and interpret the data in a scholarly manner.
   (C) Members of the general public lack the motivation and dedication to conduct scientific research. They may not follow through and complete their part of the research which would therefore, skew the results.
   (D) Some projects may not be suitable for volunteers, for instance when they use complex research methods or require arduous or repetitive work.

3. Which of the following are examples of how the automatic collection of data by computers and/or mobile devices creates privacy and/or security issues?

   I. Many people choose to sell their old computer or mobile device equipment in order to make some money or upgrade to a new device. Unless the device is properly wiped clean (which is rarely done), the purchaser may be able to access all of the previous owners personal information.

   II. Some computers have added fingerprint scanners to keep a user protected from identity theft. Unfortunately, when that device is stolen, the thief now has access to a user's fingerprint, making the identity theft more all-encompassing.

   III. Cookies on your browser can pose threats in several ways. Because cookies store information about you and send information back and forth from the servers every time you visit a site, they can cause both types of problems. Many cookies store sign on and payment information for e-commerce sites. They don't ask for verification so anyone with access to the computer would have the ability to make purchases posing as someone else.

   IV. One of the newest tools to become available are programs that allow a user to log in once and, in turn, have the application or program log them in to all of their password-protected sites that they have added to the single sign-on tool (banking, social media, home security, etc.). Should the device or just the login information for the single sign-on site find its way into the hands of a criminal, all of person's information can be obtained from one simple login.

   (A) I and III only
   (B) II and IV only
   (C) I, III and IV only
   (D) All of the above

4. John is a teacher who travels to developing countries during the summer to teach the local children. He is trying to figure out a way that his students in the United States can help him facilitate lessons with their peers in places like Guatemala, Haiti, and the Dominican Republic. John has 15 tablet devices and 5 cell phones that he can take on his trip. He will have Wi-Fi access at all of his destinations. Select the option below that best describes how John's students can contribute the most to his lessons.
    (A) John's students can use the cloud to save slideshow presentations on various subjects that the students in the foreign countries will be able to access and view. John can use the translation options on his devices for the native languages of the foreign students.
    (B) John can ask some of his students to be available at specified dates over the summer so they can interact with their foreign counterparts in real time and use their devices to show what life is like in the U.S. for students their age through videos, music, etc.
    (C) John's students can come up with a list of mobile apps and websites that the foreign students can access during John's travels. John can tell the foreign students that they are using apps chosen by his students.
    (D) John can have his students make videos of themselves teaching lessons on their favorite subjects. John can then show the videos to the foreign students so they can have John's students as their teachers.

5. Research projects can involve countless hours of tedious work. Now, however, by utilizing the knowledge of Internet users, scientists and other researchers can work more quickly through many processes that before would have taken weeks, months, or years. Review the list below and choose the project that is least likely to benefit from crowdsourcing (enlisting the help of multiple people via the web to work on a particular task).
    (A) Identifying the chemical components of various liquids found in unlabeled containers at closed industrial facilities
    (B) Annotating the diaries of soldiers from WWI
    (C) Using pictures from camera traps to identify and catalog wild animals
    (D) Providing free language learning resources by way of translating various public documents

6. The economics and business of Internet access is a process that most users do not ever think about (until their service is interrupted). Providing access to the infrastructure that is necessary for people to use the Internet is done through a process known as what?
    (A) Asset Allocation
    (B) Peering
    (C) Apportionment
    (D) Transitioning

7. Bob is a high school freshman and a budding Egyptologist. He wants to learn all he can about ancient Egyptian culture. Review the choices below and select the one that would be the most efficient method for Bob to find verified, scholarly information regarding Egyptology.

(A) Use an online search engine to do a search for Egyptology websites. Once a list is generated, go through each site to determine its validity and the extent of its viable resources.

(B) Go to the local library and look for books and reference materials that are available either in that library or in other collections in the regional library network.

(C) Using email, contact prominent Egyptologists from around the world and ask them for information and/or advice on how to find Egyptology resources.

(D) Utilize the numerous online databases that are specific to Egyptology. They provide access to peer-reviewed journals and research immediately.

8. While the Internet and the World Wide Web are now common in the workplace, many people worry that digital tools can be a distraction to workers. Employees, on the other hand, do not agree. Below are some reasons why workers feel that their productivity is not impacted by Internet technology. Which of the following are true?

I. The number of people outside of the company that workers need to communicate with is expanding.

II. Employees have more flexibility in the hours they work with the availability of working remotely.

III. The amount of hours worked by employees with digital tools has increased.

IV. The speed and accuracy with which work is completed has improved with technology.

(A) II & III
(B) II & IV
(C) I, II, & IV
(D) I, II, III & IV

9. In 2014 it was reported that a machine learning algorithm was being applied in Art History to study fine art paintings. After reviewing many paintings, it was reported that the algorithm may have revealed previously unrecognized influences between artists. Which of the options below that are also applications of machine learning? Select two answers.

(A) A program that scrapes data from various websites and organizes it based on the websites the data was collected from.

(B) A medical diagnostic program that contains vast amounts of medical data and can do fast, fact-based analyses of a patient's symptoms

(C) A robot locomotion program that analyzes all known routes and locomotor methods and creates a route that is the most efficient

(D) A linear analysis of the statistics related to a telecom company's shrinking customer base.

10. When people surf the web, they are giving out almost as much information as they are taking in. This information can be used by online advertisers to ensure that you are seeing ads that are relevant and that you are more likely to click on. Which of the following activities would NOT allow online advertising companies to target you with specific ads?

    (A) Steve goes to an online shopping site and makes selections that fill his online shopping cart. However, he decides against making the purchase and empties the cart before checking out.

    (B) Megan is shopping for a new computer and is reading online articles and product comparisons to look for the best deal.

    (C) Jim has done a search for some fishing gear he wants to buy. He clicks on some of the sponsored links that take him to fishing equipment sites but he never selects any products to look at.

    (D) Nicole logs into her email and notices that she has received several emails from a travel agency. She deletes the emails before opening them as she is not planning a trip anytime soon.

11. As mobile computing technology has exploded, many things that were normally the purview of the desktop computer have gone mobile. Which of the following scenarios below are examples of tasks that have moved from the desktop to the mobile world?

    I.   During a business trip, a project manager uses her smart phone to teleconference with her production team from the airport.

    II. A high school student uses real-time, location-specific texting and chat apps on his cell phone to talk to his friends.

    III. Avid football fans on their way to a game are stuck in a train station so they stream the game to their tablet.

    IV. A passer-by witnesses a fire breaking out at an industrial plant. She uses her phone to take videos and post them to her social media sites.

    (A) I, III
    (B) II, III, IV
    (C) I, III, IV
    (D) I, II, III, & IV

12. Alvy Ray Smith, the co-founder of Pixar, has written an article discussing the evolution of Pixar. In his article he states that forty years ago he and his colleagues conceived the idea of a fully digital movie. It took 20 more years to finally have the technology that allowed for the creation of *Toy Story*. What concept in computing gave Smith and his colleagues the belief that in time, the technology would evolve to the level needed by Pixar to create their first digital movie?

    (A) Hollerith's Principle
    (B) Moore's Law
    (C) Hopper's Theorem
    (D) Murphy's Formula

13. When legally purchasing a physical music CD or movie DVD, a concept known as the first sale doctrine is invoked. This doctrine determines what can and can't be done with that physical item. The first sale doctrine does not apply to legal digital downloads. Which of the following scenarios IS allowed for most legal digital downloads?

(A) Your friend can plug their digital music player into your laptop and copy music onto it that you have legally purchased.

(B) You can put digital music files on multiple machines and/or devices that you own.

(C) You can view downloaded video files on multiple machines simultaneously and you may move them from device to device.

(D) You can transfer your purchases to another person and they will retain all of the same rights you had.

14. Which of the following are computing methods that contribute to the development and implementation, or are examples of, assistive technologies?

I. A mechanical engineer uses CAD software to design a prosthetic leg.

II. A surgeon implants a pacemaker to control a heart arrhythmia.

III. A student with a visual impairment utilizes headphones and a screen reader.

IV. A person confined to a wheelchair uses voice commands to navigate the web.

(A) I, II

(B) I, III

(C) II, IV

(D) I, III, IV

15. Web surfing anonymizers (a form of proxy server) are very prevalent on the web today. Many people feel that these anonymizers/proxy servers are used to hide Internet activities from schools, employers, parents, etc. However, there are some valid reasons for using an anonymizer/proxy server. Which of the following is NOT a valid reason?

(A) A web surfer can prevent identify theft if they use anonymizers when using personal data online and the anonymizer uses SSL or SSH encryption.

(B) Anonymizers allow people to surf the web and avoid targeted marketing based on cookies and other location services.

(C) Anonymizers allow people to avoid detection for all of their Internet activities including searches, purchases, chats sessions, etc.

(D) Web browsing history is protected as your IP address is not relayed to the sites you are visiting.

Answers

1. **Answer: B.** While this scenario seems like it could be true and while there are many people who use the Internet to research cold cases, this story is false as no "confirmed identity" has ever been made.

Learning Objectives	Essential Knowledge
LO 7.1.2 Explain how people participate in a problem-solving process that scales.	**EK 7.1.2E** Some online services use the contributions of many people to benefit both individuals and society.

2. **Answers: B, C.** Although the concept of citizen science is very new, there has been research conducted about it. This research shows that the limitations that exist have to do with observer bias and methodology.

Learning Objectives	Essential Knowledge
LO 7.1.2 Explain how people participate in a problem-solving process that scales.	**EK 7.1.2B** Science has been impacted by using scale and "citizen science" to solve scientific problems using home computers in scientific research.

3. **Answer C.** All of these examples, with the exception of II, are methods in which data collected on your computer and/or mobile device (knowingly or unknowingly) can cause privacy or security issues.

Learning Objectives	Essential Knowledge
LO 7.3.1 Analyze the beneficial and harmful effects of computing.	**EK 7.3.1H** Aggregation of information, such as geolocation, cookies, and browsing history, raises privacy and security concerns.

4. **Answer: B.** To fully utilize the capabilities of the devices that he has, John should actively engage both his own students and the foreign students he is working with. By doing so, both sets of students will benefit and learn about each other.

Learning Objectives	Essential Knowledge
LO 7.4.1 Explain the connections between computing and real-world contexts, including economic, social, and cultural contexts.	**EK 7.4.1B** Mobile, wireless, and networked computing have an impact on innovation throughout the world. **EK 7.4.1C** The global distribution of computing resources raises issues of equity, access, and power.

5. **Answer: A.** the other three options are all actual human computation opportunities. In order to do an accurate analysis of a chemical composition, you would need to be present to conduct the experiment. You could review the findings online or remotely, but the actual experiment would be done in person.

Learning Objectives	Essential Knowledge
LO 7.1.2 Explain how people participate in a problem-solving process that scales.	EK 7.1.2C Human computation harnesses contributions from many humans to solve problems related to digital data and the Web.

6. **Answer: B.** The backbone of the Internet is built on peering and transit agreements. Peering is a voluntary interconnection of separate networks by separate entities for the purpose of sharing traffic (and therefore the burden of usage) across the entirety of the network.

Learning Objectives	Essential Knowledge
LO 7.4.1 Explain the connections between computing and real-world contexts, including economic, social, and cultural contexts.	EK 7.4.1E Networks and infrastructure are supported by both commercial and governmental initiatives.

7. **Answer: D.** While all of the selections are valid, choice D is the most efficient method for obtaining the information Bob is looking for. The level of information along with its immediacy and constant availability make it the best choice.

Learning Objectives	Essential Knowledge
LO 7.2.1 Explain how computing has impacted innovations in other fields.	EK 7.2.1E Open and curated scientific databases have benefited scientific researchers.

8. **Answer: D.** All of these responses are valid, positive impacts of the Internet and technology on productivity.

Learning Objectives	Essential Knowledge
LO 7.1.1 Explain how computing innovations affect communication, interaction and cognition.	EK 7.1.1O The Internet and the Web have impacted productivity, positively and negatively, in many areas.

9. **Answers: B, C.** The fields of machine learning, data mining, statistical modeling, and artificial intelligence are all very closely related. However, the question specifically asks for example of machine learning. Answers B&C are both predictive in nature which is the hallmark of machine learning.

Learning Objectives	Essential Knowledge
LO 7.2.1 Explain how computing has impacted innovations in other fields.	EK 7.2.1A Machine learning and data mining have enabled innovation in medicine, business, and science.

10. **Answers: D**. All of the other options will allow online advertisers to gather the information they want in order to target advertising directly for you. Much of this is one in the form of cookies. Choice D is the best choice since receiving the emails indicates the user was already targeted and not opening them ensures that additional personal information is not sent.

Learning Objectives	Essential Knowledge
LO 7.3.1 Analyze the beneficial and harmful effects of computing.	**EK 7.3.1J** Technology enables the collection, use, and exploitation of information about, by, and for individuals, groups, and institutions. **EK 7.3.1M** Targeted advertising is used to help individuals but it can be misused at both individual and aggregate levels.

11. **Answer: C**. All of these activities (teleconferencing, streaming video, and updating social media originally had to be done via a desktop or laptop computer. Nowadays, all of these can be done via smart phone or tablet. Option II is incorrect as the types of apps described are specific to cell phones or tablets.

Learning Objectives	Essential Knowledge
LO 7.1.2 Explain how people participate in a problem-solving process that scales.	**EK 7.1.2G** The move from desktop computers to a proliferation of always-on mobile computers is leading to new applications.

12. **Answer: B**. Moore's law, as originally stated by Gordon Moore in 1965 and revised in 1975, says that the number of transistors in an integrated circuit would double every two years. Alvy Smith states it as "Everything good about computers gets an order of magnitude better every five years". This "law" has proven to be accurate even 50 years after its creation.

Learning Objectives	Essential Knowledge
LO 7.2.1 Explain how computing has impacted innovations in other fields.	**EK 7.2.1F** Moore's Law has encouraged industries that use computers to effectively plan future research and development based on anticipated increases in computing power.

13. **Answer: B**. Based on reviewing the policies of Apple, Amazon, and Google, the only option above that is allowable is to put downloaded music files on multiple devices. All of the other scenarios listed are violations of digital user agreements.

Learning Objectives	Essential Knowledge
LO 7.3.1 Analyze the beneficial and harmful effects of computing.	**EK 7.3.1B** Commercial access to music and movie downloads and streaming raises legal and ethical concerns.

14. **Answer: D.** By definition, a surgically implanted device is not considered an assistive technology.

Learning Objectives	Essential Knowledge
LO 7.1.1 Explain how computing innovations affect communication, interaction, and cognition.	**EK 7.1.1L** Computing contributes to many assistive technologies that enhance human capabilities.

15. **Answer: C.** While on the surface this might seem like a benefit, allowing people to avoid all detection on the web allows for the potential of illegal and/or illicit activities and make it difficult for authorities to locate the offender.

Learning Objectives	Essential Knowledge
LO 7.3.1 Analyze the beneficial and harmful effects of computing.	**EK 7.3.1D** Both authenticated and anonymous access to digital information raise legal and ethical concerns.

Part III

Practice Tests

Practice Test 1

AP® Computer Science Principles Examination
Time: 120 minutes
Number of questions: 74

DIRECTIONS: Each of the questions below is followed by four suggested answers. For each question select the best response. For multiple-select questions, choose the two best responses.

1. Bytes, which are represented by 8 bits, are the units used by computers to represent a character such as a letter or number. The following characters are shown with their decimal representations:

C	67
K	75
.	96
p	112

   Which of the above, represented in binary as a byte, contains the most zeros?
   (A) C
   (B) K
   (C) .
   (D) p

2. We can convert a number from decimal to octal (base 8) by repeatedly subtracting the largest possible powers of what number?
   (A) 2
   (B) 7
   (C) 8
   (D) 9

3. The question below uses a simple programming language, with the following instructions.

```
product ← 100
REPEAT 1000 TIMES
{
  product ← product * product + 1
}
```

   In some coding languages, the above code will result in an error. Why?
   (A) The fixed number of bits used to represent real numbers (as floating-point numbers) limits the range of floating-point values and mathematical operations.
   (B) The multiple levels of abstraction used oversimplified the code.
   (C) The value of product will always be 0.
   (D) The fixed number of bits used to represent characters or integers limits the range of integer values and mathematical operations.

125

4. A customer is shopping online, and purchases a product advertised at $10.99. She has a 40% discount, bringing the price to $6.594 each. She decided to purchase 3. Her final total should be $19.78, but the total instead is $19.77. Choose <u>the most likely</u> possible explanation for the discrepancy:
   (A) The program calculating the total rounded the price for one of the products, then multiplied by 3.
   (B) While multiplying the floating point numbers, there was a round-off error.
   (C) The fixed number of bits used to store the values resulted in an overflow error.
   (D) The program does not handle signed integers.

5. Sort the following by levels of abstraction, from lowest to highest:
   I.   logic gates
   II. operating systems
   III. programming language
   IV. machine language

   (A) I, II, III, IV
   (B) I, III, IV, II
   (C) I, IV, II, III
   (D) I, IV, III, II

6. Which of the following statements are true about high-level programming languages? Select <u>two</u> answers.
   (A) A high-level programming language often uses natural language elements.
   (B) A high-level programming language does not ensure program reliability.
   (C) A high-level programming language must be used to execute commands such adding and multiplying.
   (D) A high-level program language allows for code re-use.

7. Which of the following statements is NOT correct:
   (A) Logic gates are used to perform operations such as addition and subtraction.
   (B) Logic gates are modeled by Boolean functions.
   (C) Hardware is the lowest level of abstraction.
   (D) Binary data is processed by physical layers of computing hardware.

8. Consider the goal of flipping two fair coins simultaneously three times and displaying the number of times both coins land on the same values (heads or tails). Which of the following code segments can be used to accomplish that goal? Select <u>two</u> answers.

(A)
```
count ← 0
REPEAT 3 TIMES
{
    IF (RANDOM(0,1) = RANDOM(0,1))
    {
        count ← count + 1
    }
}
DISPLAY count
```

(B)
```
count ← 0
REPEAT 3 TIMES
{
    IF (RANDOM(1,2) = RANDOM(1,2))
    {
        count ← count + 1
    }
}
DISPLAY count
```

(C)
```
REPEAT 3 TIMES
{
    count ← 0
    IF (RANDOM(0,1) = RANDOM(0,1))
    {
        count ← count + 1
    }
}
DISPLAY count
```

(D)
```
count ← 0
REPEAT 3 TIMES
{
    IF (RANDOM(0,2) = RANDOM(0,2))
    {
        count ← count + 1
    }
}
DISPLAY count
```

9. Consider the procedure mystery (num, list):

```
PROCEDURE mystery (num, list)
{
  FOR EACH item IN list
  {
        if (list [item] MOD num == 0)
  {
        DISPLAY list[item] + " "
  REMOVE list[item]
        }
  }
}
```

If list myList contains the following data: [10, 9, 8, 7, 6, 5, 4, 3, 2, 1, 0], what will be displayed by mystery (3, myList) ?

(A) 10 8 7 5 4 2 1
(B) 10 8 7 5 4 2 1 0
(C) 9 6 3
(D) 9 6 3 0

10. Consider the following procedure, cube (n), which is meant to multiply a number by itself three times.

```
PROCEDURE cube (n)
{
  cubeValue ← n * n * n
  RETURN (cubeValue)
}
```

What is the returned by cube (cube (2))?

(A) 8
(B) 64
(C) 128
(D) 512

11. Consider the following procedure, mystery (x, y).

```
PROCEDURE mystery (x, y)
{
        IF (x < 2)
  {
        x ← 2
  }
  IF (x < 2)
  {
        y ← x + 3
  }
  RETURN (x * y)
}
```

What is the returned by mystery (1, 2)?

(A) 2
(B) 4
(C) 8
(D) 10

12. In researching a local deer population, a scientist has gathered much information about the deer and is going to write a program to model population growth over time. She wants to analyze how illness and population size are related to available food sources. Which of the following factors most likely does <u>not</u> need to be included in her program:
    (A) Population size
    (B) Food supply
    (C) Antler size
    (D) Prevalence of illness in herd

13. Consider a computer simulation of a deck of 52 cards, with face values from 1 to 13. Every value appears on four cards, each of a different suit, with the suits assigned values of 1 to 4. The following procedure represents choosing a card at random.

```
PROCEDURE choose()
{
face ← RANDOM(1, 13)
suit ← RANDOM (1, 4)
DISPLAY (face + " of " + suit)
}
```

What could the following code segment potentially be modelling?

```
REPEAT 5 TIMES
{
    choose()
}
```

(A) A card dealer deals a five-card hand to one player.
(B) A card dealer deals one card face-up to each of five players.
(C) A card dealer turns over one card, returns it to the deck, shuffles and repeats for a total of five times.
(D) A card dealer gives one card each to five players, repeating a total of five times until each player holds five cards.

14. A word cloud is an image made of words which vary in size based on their frequency or importance. A literature teacher is exploring the overuse of the word "that" in her students' writing. The students disagree with the teacher, so the teacher creates a word cloud for each student from their essays to visually demonstrate the frequency of the word "that." What are some possible outcomes of this exploration?
    I.   The teacher may realize there are, in fact, other words overused by her students.
    II. The teacher may find other words the students use frequently with the word "that", and can help the students find new appropriate expressions.
    III. The teacher may decide to study the issue further, and test individual paragraphs in the students' works, or may decide to test all of their essays in one word cloud.

    (A) I and II
    (B) I and III
    (C) II and III
    (D) I, II, and III

15. The DARPA Robotics Challenge (DRC) is a prize competition funded by the US Defense Advanced Research Projects Agency. It aims to develop semi-autonomous ground robots that can perform a variety of tasks. Some of the tasks the robots must complete are driving a vehicle through a course, opening a door, turning a valve, independent movement, and navigating debris. What scientific fields would need to be represented on a team that is trying to win the DRC?
    (A) Computer science, mechanical engineering, biology, electronics, and remote systems
    (B) Mechanical engineering, biology, and computer science
    (C) Computer science, electronics, remote systems, and biology
    (D) Remote systems, computer science, and mechanical engineering

16. In the digital world we live in, collaboration is critical. People must be able to work as members of a functional team in order to get things accomplished. Whether the collaboration is taking place in a conference room or a virtual world, there are some tenets about collaboration that ring true. Which of the following is true of effective collaboration?
    I.   Synergy is created in the midst of collaboration.
    II. Trust relationships are built and enhanced.
    III. Projects are completed more timely and efficiently.
    IV. An effective leader can mold quality team members to fit his or her style.
    V.   Collaborative team members must know the limits of what they can deliver.

    (A) I, III, and IV only
    (B) II, IV, & V only
    (C) I, II, III, and V only
    (D) All of the above

17. In the past, the lack of data was a hindrance to scientific discovery. Today, the opposite is true. It is not the lack of data that is the problem; the issue is how to work with the vast amounts of data that are available. Scientists must know how to manage, share, and analyze very large data sets. Which of the following statements are NOT true of scientists using large datasets? Select two answers.
   (A) The costs associated with medical advancements are reduced due to large scale collaboration on the data.
   (B) Effectively analyzing the large, complex datasets requires abilities beyond the skill sets possessed by a single scientist.
   (C) Scientists using large data sets are more effective in their research when they limit the amount of data they analyze in a collaborative group.
   (D) A team of people from various disciplines increases the complexity of the analysis that is being done.

18. A digital art teacher has her students analyze a digital image to get the RGB values of each pixel that is present in the image. The teacher provides them with a program that gathers the RGB values in a triplet for each pixel—for example (255, 124, 36)—and loads them into a data set. The data set is then imported into a spreadsheet program so that the pixel number is in column A, the R value is in column B, G value in column C, and B value in column D. The students will do an analysis of the RGB values to determine which series of values is used most often. Which of the algorithms below would allow the student to create an analysis that accomplishes the task?
   I. Sort the RGB triplets by R value (ascending or descending). Once that is done find the R value that occurs the most and remove any triplets that do not include that value. Re-sort the list by G values. Count the G value that occurs the most and remove any triplets that do not include that value. Re-sort the remaining list by the B values. Count the B value that occurs the most and remove any triplets that do not include that value. The remaining RBG triplet is the one that occurs most often.
   II. Sort the RGB triplets in descending order by the R value first, followed by the G value and then the B value. Once that has been done, iterate across the list to find the triplets that have the highest count of R values. Create a new list of the triplets that have the highest R value count. Iterate across that list to find the highest count of G values and create a new list of triplets, remove the remaining triplets. Do the same for the B values. That will leave the RGB triplet that occurs most often.

   (A) I only
   (B) II only
   (C) Both I & II
   (D) Neither I & II

19. Amelia is doing a research paper on wild animals of the Americas. She wants to include some research on the wild mustangs of the west. Which of the search terms below would give her the most specific information on the topic she is searching for? Select <u>two</u> answers.
    (A) Mustang -car
    (B) "Mustang, not the car"
    (C) Mustang NOT car
    (D) Site: Mustang

20. Zach has just finished watching his favorite movie on a streaming site. As the movie is coming to a close, the screen splits and Zach is shown a list of recommended movies to watch next. The streaming site that Zach is watching is using what type of system to make the suggestions?
    (A) Preference categorization
    (B) Statistical probability model
    (C) Reference grouping
    (D) Information filtering

21. Protecting personal privacy in large data sets is an ever-growing concern. Which of the following methods below can be used to mitigate the risk of possibly releasing personally identifiable information in large data sets?
    I.   Aggregation – changing atypical records into typical records (e.g., making all last names the same)
    II. Suppression – deleting identifying values from the data (e.g., no addresses)
    III. Data Swapping – change the values for pieces of data (e.g., swap age values for ethnic values, etc.)
    IV. Adding Random Noise – including meaningless values in the data (e.g., adding extra digits to phone numbers)
    V.   Key Master – ensuring that no more than one person in an organization has complete access to a database

    (A) I, II, and IV only
    (B) II, IV, and V only
    (C) I, II, III, and IV only
    (D) All of the above

22. Managing digital data involves many considerations. Among these are security and privacy. Review the scenarios below. Which pose valid security concerns? Select <u>two</u> answers.
    (A) A government contractor is on a business trip and attempts to transfer files. His files are too large for his email account, so he creates an account in the cloud to store his file until he gets back to work, where he can retrieve it.
    (B) A bank customer is using an online banking site to pay bills and transfer funds across accounts. The customer is using his wireless system at home that hides the SSID from the public.
    (C) An employee receives a call from a person stating that they are with the company's IT department. The caller states that they are in the process of updating the server and needs the employee's username and password.
    (D) A company wants to get rid of old, extraneous customer data. Rather than physically destroying its old hard drives, it follows government and industry standard protocols for permanent data erasure.

23. Lossless and lossy compression are present in many different file formats (image, music, video, etc.). The graphic below illustrates how the two compression formats work.

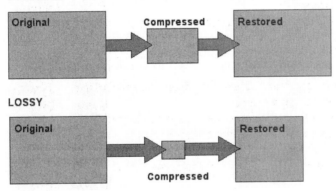

Which of the following statements below is NOT true?
    (A) All lossless compression is based on the idea of breaking a file into a smaller form for transmission or storage and then being put back together in its entirety.
    (B) Lossy formats are excellent to use when a file must be compressed and rebuilt to its exact pre-compressed specifications.
    (C) Scanning in a picture creates a lossy format result. The program gives you its interpretation of the original.
    (D) Moving music onto your digital music player is done is a lossless format to reduce the size of the file.

24. Metadata is defined as data about data. Review the following statements about metadata types. Which of the statements below are true.
    I. Descriptive metadata is used for discovery and identification (e.g., a title, subject, or keyword)
    II. Administrative metadata gives information to help identify the source (e.g., file type, or when file was created).
    III. Metadata automatically generated tends to be more accurate than manually created metadata.
    IV. Structural metadata describes how the components are organized (e.g., the chapters of a book).

    (A) I only
    (B) II III, and IV only
    (C) I, II, and IV only
    (D) All of the above

25. When scientists, engineers, businesses, etc. are working with large data sets, they consider many factors in choosing a storage method for their data. Some of these include cost, accessibility, and mobility. Which of the following storage methods below makes accessibility of data easiest for people in multiple locations wanting to utilize the data?
    (A) USB Flash Drive, as it can be copied and handed or mailed to multiple users.
    (B) Mainframe Computer, as it can be accessed from many computers.
    (C) Cloud Drive, as it allows for multiple users and version control.
    (D) Magnetic Drive System, as it can handle all data types.

26. Five friends are planning a biking trip in Boston, and want to know how many covered bike racks are available along the city's Freedom Trail. They are specifically looking for bike racks large enough to accommodate all five bikes. The friends have a list with the following information for each bike rack:
    - location along the trail
    - whether the rack is covered or uncovered
    - the number of bikes that the rack can hold

    Which algorithm, if any, can the friends use to find the number of covered bike racks along the Freedom Trail to accommodate all five of them?
    I. Algorithm I: Filter the data by creating a new list of only bike racks that have parking for more than four bikes. Set a counter equal to 0. Iterate through the sorted list of spots. If the spot is covered, add 1 to count.
    II. Algorithm II: Set a counter equal to 0. Filter the data by creating a new list of only bike racks that are covered. Iterate through the list of covered spots. Every time a spot has a capacity of greater than 4, add 1 to the counter.

    (A) I only
    (B) II only
    (C) Both I and II
    (D) Neither I nor II

27. A mother is attempting to determine which cell phone plan best fits her family's needs. She plans on using a shared pool of data for everyone in her family (defined as the people living in her home). Identify the best sequence of steps she should take to select a plan.
    I.   Determine each family member's data usage.
    II.   If the cost for data overages is lower than the added cost of the next tiered plan, select the plan with about the same amount of data that the family uses. Otherwise, select the plan with slightly more data than the family uses.
    III. Find the sum of the total data usage for each member of the family.
    IV.   Compare the cost of paying for data overages to the cost of paying for slightly more data.

    (A) I, II, III, IV
    (B) III, I, II, IV
    (C) I, IV, II, III
    (D) I, III, IV, II

28. A color can be represented with 3 bytes of information. A BMP image stores image information by storing the individual color at each pixel. On the other hand, a GIF image stores a table of colors, and replaces runs of consecutive occurrences of the same color with (#ofOccurances, color) pairs. Both BMP and GIF are lossless formats. Which format is more efficient for storing and representing most images and why?
    (A) GIF. Storing the data in pairs allow us only to use the 3 bytes once for each set of consecutive colors.
    (B) GIF. Storing information in a table format ensures losslessness.
    (C) BMP. The algorithm for storing a BMP file has fewer steps.
    (D) BMP. Having access to the data at every pixel ensures losslessness.

29. A game designer is creating a new online card game where the player's hand becomes larger over time. The game is played with multiple decks of cards. Once all cards have been distributed to all players, the software will sort through each player's cards and put them in order by suit and face value. What strategies can the designer use to find an efficient sorting algorithm? Select <u>two</u> answers.
    (A) The designer can find an efficient algorithm for sorting the cards in one player's hand, early in the game, and build on that algorithm as the game becomes larger and involves more players.
    (B) The designer can use pre-existing sorting methods and modify them to suit his own work.
    (C) The designer can try to reduce his code to as few lines as possible.
    (D) The designer can host the game on a large server.

30. What are the two aspects of efficiency?
    (A) execution time and memory usage
    (B) memory usage and length of code
    (C) execution time and length of code
    (D) wall clock time and CPU time

31. A lawyer is accessing an online database of crimes within a certain radius of the city center. The database contains the following information:
    ▨ Date of crime
    ▨ Name of offenders
    ▨ Neighborhood of crime

    The lawyer is looking for other crimes that occurred in a certain area on a certain date. Which of the following algorithms can he use to find all crimes that occurred in a certain neighborhood on a certain day?
    I. Make a new list by filtering the data so only the crimes from a certain neighborhood are on the list. Perform multiple binary searches to find all crimes that occurred on the given day, adding each new occurrence to a final list.
    II. Make a new list by filtering the data so only the crimes from a certain neighborhood are on the list. Perform multiple linear searches to find all crimes that occurred on the given day, adding each new occurrence to a final list.

    (A) Algorithm I only
    (B) Algorithm II only
    (C) Both Algorithms I and Algorithm II
    (D) Neither Algorithm I nor Algorithm II

32. A programming language that is <u>dynamically typed</u> determines a variable's data type (i.e., string, float, etc.) at runtime. A language that is <u>statically typed</u> (not dynamic), must declare its variable types when written. With dynamically typed languages, the code runs slower, as the computer is determining data types at runtime. What are the best reasons for choosing one language over another? Select <u>two</u> answers.
    (A) A programmer uses a statically typed language because she knows that her program will use a lot of memory, and she wants to reduce runtime.
    (B) A programmer uses a statically typed language because she wants her variable declarations to be clear to those reviewing and revising her code, without unnecessary comments.
    (C) A programmer uses a dynamically typed language because it is the current trend and she feels she will earn more money using a trendy language.
    (D) A programmer uses a dynamically typed language because her program has a large number of calculations with various data types, and she does not want to have to worry about data-type compatibility while writing her program.

33. Consider an algorithm that simulates rolling two number cubes, Cube1 and Cube2, with the numbers 1 – 6, and then displays the sum of the two cubes' values. If the sum is greater than 10, "Winner!" is also displayed; otherwise, "Loser" is displayed. Put the steps of the algorithm in order. Select <u>two</u> answers.

Step 1:   Assign random values between 1 and 6 to Cube1.

Step 2:   If sum is greater than 10, display "Winner!".

Step 3:   Display sum.

Step 4:   If the sum is less than or equal to 10, display "Loser".

Step 5:   Assign random values between 1 and 6 to Cube2.

Step 6:   Assign the value of Cube1 + Cube2 to sum.

(A) Step 1, Step 5, Step 6, Step 3, Step 4, Step 2
(B) Step 5, Step 1, Step 6, Step 3, Step 2, Step 4
(C) Step 5, Step 1, Step 2,Step 4, Step 6, Step 3
(D) Step 1, Step 5, Step 3, Step 6, Step 2, Step 4

34. An online dating website has a list of users that has been sorted alphabetically by last name. In order to find a certain user, a binary search is performed. As many new members are added to the database, will the number of steps the algorithm will take to solve the problem <u>most likely</u> also increase? Why or why not?
(A) Yes, the number of steps in an algorithm changes proportional to the size of the input.
(B) Yes, because the new members may not be added alphabetically.
(C) No, the program is written already, and will take the same number of steps regardless of the size of the database.
(D) No, because the search is binary, so the dataset is split in half with every iteration.

35. A shipping service company is attempting to create a route for truck drivers for last-minute holiday deliveries. Given the impending deadline, the company's programmer does not have the time to find the best route for its drivers. Identify one possible quick and reasonable solution to the problem.
(A) The programmer quickly uses software to find destinations close to each other and draw out reasonable routes to get through the holidays.
(B) The programmer relies on the knowledge and experience of the drivers, and counts on them to plan their own routes.
(C) The programmer delays the drivers, knowing that he will save time in the long run by holding back deliveries until he finds the perfect solution.
(D) The programmer writes new code, attempting to solve the problem in new ways despite the impending deadline.

36. An online museum is creating a site hosting hundreds of thousands of digital representations of art from around the world. They want to use a lossless compression, so that members of the museum can download and decompress the image and have an identical copy of the original file. Which of the following are true? Select <u>two</u> answers.
    (A) The museum should not compress digital representations of art, as there is always a danger that the compression is actually lossy.
    (B) The museum can choose a heuristic approach which will achieve a lossless compression, but they cannot be sure that it is the most efficient compression for each image.
    (C) The museum can choose a heuristic approach which will achieve a lossless compression for most digital representations.
    (D) Algorithms for lossless compression exist, so the museum can use those to compress the images.

37. Consider the following complicated program, which is intended to move the robot from the top left hand corner of the empty grid, facing east, to the lower right hand corner of the grid, facing east:

    Before:

    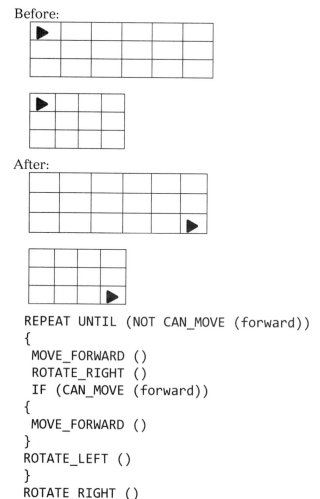

    After:

```
REPEAT UNTIL (NOT CAN_MOVE (forward))
{
  MOVE_FORWARD ()
  ROTATE_RIGHT ()
  IF (CAN_MOVE (forward))
  {
  MOVE_FORWARD ()
  }
  ROTATE_LEFT ()
}
ROTATE_RIGHT ()
REPEAT UNTIL (NOT CAN_MOVE (forward))
```

```
{
  MOVE_FORWARD ()
}
ROTATE_LEFT ()
```

Which of the following less complicated code segments could replace the above code and will result in the correct final position of the robot?

I.
```
REPEAT UNTIL (NOT CAN_MOVE (forward))
{
  MOVE_FORWARD ()
  ROTATE_RIGHT ()
  MOVE_FORWARD ()
  ROTATE_LEFT ()
}
```

II.
```
REPEAT UNTIL (NOT CAN_MOVE (forward))
{
  MOVE_FORWARD ()
}
ROTATE_RIGHT ()
REPEAT UNTIL (NOT CAN_MOVE (forward))
{
  MOVE_FORWARD ()
}
ROTATE_LEFT ()
```

(A) I only
(B) II only
(C) I and II
(D) Neither I nor II

38. An entrepreneur gave her customers a survey, asking them to rate various aspects of a new product on a scale of 1 to 5. The integer values of their answers were stored in list feedback. Which code segments would assign the correct value to average? Select <u>two</u> answers.

    (A)
    ```
    sum ← 0
    FOR EACH item IN feedback
    {
            sum ← sum + item
    }
    average ← sum / LENGTH(feedback)
    ```

    (B)
    ```
    FOR EACH item IN feedback
    {
            sum ← 0
      sum ← sum + item
    }
    average ← sum / LENGTH(feedback)
    ```

    (C)
    ```
    sum ← 0
    REPEAT LENGTH(feedback) times
     {
       sum ← sum + item
     }
    average ← sum / LENGTH(feedback)
    ```

    (D)
    ```
    sum ← 0
      item ← 1
    REPEAT LENGTH(feedback) times
     {
       sum ← sum + list[item]
       item ← item + 1
     }
    average ← sum / LENGTH(feedback)
    ```

39. A student writes a program to find the factorial of a number. The factorial for a number n is defined as the product of all whole numbers between 1 and n, inclusive. While attempting to find the factorial for 120, the program's output is not what the student expected. Assuming that the program has been correctly written, what is a possible explanation for the incorrect output?

    (A) Real numbers are approximated by floating-point representations that do not necessarily have infinite precision.

    (B) Integers may be constrained in the maximum and minimum values that can be represented in a program because of storage limitations.

    (C) Factorials are an antiquated concept, and modern program languages do not have the operations available to handle them.

    (D) Although correct, the program did not make use of procedures, which made it unstable.

40. A landscaper wants to write a program to calculate the area of circle (Area = pi * radius * radius) where a pool will be placed so he can use that area to help him calculate how much grass seed he should purchase for the entire lawn. Which one of the following factors does he need to take into consideration while writing the program?
(A) He needs to make sure that the language he chooses uses the necessary arithmetic operators.
(B) The height of the pool must be taken into account so the volume (Volume = Area * height) can be incorporated into the calculations.
(C) Because pi is an irrational number, it will have to be approximated by a floating-point representation, such as 3.1, 3.14, or 3.142, depending on the accuracy needed.
(D) A Boolean expression should be included in the program to determine whether or not a pool actually exists.

41. Consider the goal of finding the sum of all odd integers in a list, myInts, of integers. What should replace <block of statements> to successfully find the sum of all odd integers?

```
sum ← 0;
FOR EACH num IN myInts
{
    <block of statements>
}
```

(A) `sum ← sum + num`

(B)
```
IF(NOT num MOD 2 = 0)
{
    sum ← sum + num
}
```

(C)
```
IF( myInts MOD 2 = 0)
{
    sum ← sum + myINts
}
```

(D) `sum ← sum / 2 + num`

42. Consider the following code segment:
```
IF (x > 5)
{
    x ← x + 1
}
x ← x - 1
```

What will be the value of x after this code segment executes?
(A) For all values of x, x will remain unchanged.
(B) For values greater than 5, x will remain unchanged, and for all other values, x will decrease by 1.
(C) For values greater than 5, x will increase by 1, and for all other values, x will decrease by 1.
(D) For all values of x, x will decrease by 1.

43. After the following code segment is run, what will be the values of x and y?

```
x ← 15
y ← 20
IF ( x > 10 OR y < 10)
{
  IF( x < y AND y < 30)
  {
      x ← y
      y ← x
  }
}
x ← x * 2
y ← y * 2
```

What will be the values of *x* and *y* after this code segment executes?
(A) *x* is 30, *y* is 40
(B) *x* is 20, *y* is 20
(C) *x* is 40, *y* is 30
(D) *x* is 40, *y* is 40

44. Consider the following procedure for a robot in a grid of squares:

```
PROCEDURE MYSTERY ()
{
  IF (CAN_MOVE (right))
  {
    RETURN FALSE
  }
  IF (CAN_MOVE (left))
  {
    RETURN FALSE
  }
  IF (CAN_MOVE (up))
  {
    RETURN FALSE
  }
  IF (CAN_MOVE (down))
  {
    RETURN FALSE
  }
  RETURN TRUE
}
```

What is the appropriate name for the procedure?
(A) ESCAPE ()
(B) SPIN()
(C) IS_TRAPPED ()
(D) CAN_ESCAPE()

45. Consider the following scenario and code segment for a robot in a maze of squares:

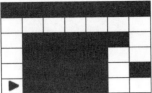

```
REPEAT UNTIL (NOT (CAN_MOVE (right) OR CAN_MOVE
(left) OR CAN_MOVE (forward) OR CAN_MOVE
(backward)))
{
  IF (CAN_MOVE(forward))
  {
    MOVE_FORWARD ()
  }
  ELSE
  {
  ROTATE_RIGHT ()
  }
}
```

Debug the above code segment. Which of the following statements is true?

(A) The code runs as intended. The robot will reach the end of the maze.

(B) The code does not run as intended. The robot will never reach the end of the maze.

(C) The code runs as intended. The code runs without error.

(D) The code may or may not run as intended. The code's purpose is not stated.

46. Consider the following incomplete code segment, with the goal of moving the robot in the grid around the obstacle.

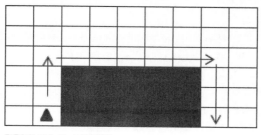

```
REPEAT 3 TIMES
{
  REPEAT UNTIL (/* missing code */)
  {
    MOVE_FORWARD ()
  }
  ROTATE_RIGHT ()
}
```

Which of the following will correctly replace /*missing code */ ?
(A) CAN_MOVE (right)
(B) NOT CAN_MOVE (right)
(C) NOT CAN_MOVE(forward)
(D) CAN_MOVE(right) AND NOT CAN_MOVE(forward)

47. Which of the following lines of code would cause an error with the robot?
(A) CAN_MOVE(right)
(B) CAN_MOVE(forward)
(C) CAN_MOVE (left)
(D) CAN_MOVE (north)

48. The Hailstone Sequence, which includes numbers that rise and fall like hailstones in a cloud, are defined by the $3n + 1$ conjecture, which states that if you follow the below algorithm, the series will always end with 1.
    Consider the algorithm below:
    Do until n is 1:
        If n is even, divide it by 2.
        Otherwise, multiply n by 3 and add 1.

Which of the following program segments correctly implements the algorithm?

(A)

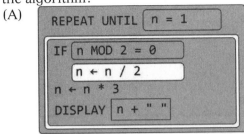

```
REPEAT UNTIL  n = 1

    IF  n MOD 2 = 0
        n ← n / 2
    n ← n * 3
    DISPLAY  n + " "
```

(B)

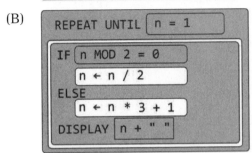

```
REPEAT UNTIL  n = 1

    IF  n MOD 2 = 0
        n ← n / 2
    ELSE
        n ← n * 3 + 1
    DISPLAY  n + " "
```

(C)

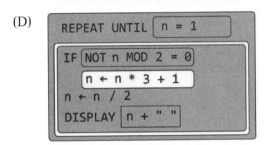

```
REPEAT UNTIL  n = 1

    IF  n MOD 2 > 0
        n ← n * 3 + 1
    n ← n / 2
    DISPLAY  n + " "
```

(D)

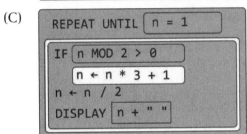

```
REPEAT UNTIL  n = 1

    IF  NOT n MOD 2 = 0
        n ← n * 3 + 1
    n ← n / 2
    DISPLAY  n + " "
```

49. The student government president is creating a mobile Android application for the dance committee to use while selling tickets for the upcoming senior formal. The following rules apply to dance ticket purchases:
   ▪ All seniors pay $20 per person.
   ▪ All non-seniors pay $30 per person.

Which of the following must be true about the code that she writes?
(A) Selection is necessary, but looping is not.
(B) Looping is necessary, but selection is not.
(C) Both selection and looping are necessary.
(D) Neither selection nor looping are necessary.

50. Consider the following code segment, meant to remove even values of item from oddList, and replace them with item + 1.

```
counter ← 1
REPEAT LENGTH (oddList) TIMES
{
  IF (oddList[counter] MOD 2 = 0)
  {
    replace_even(counter, oddList)
  }
  counter ← counter + 1
}
```

Select the replace_even(n, list) procedure that will work as intended.

(A)
```
replace_even(n, list)
{
  n ← n + 1
}
```

(B)
```
replace_even(n, list)
{
  INSERT(list, n, n + 1)
  REMOVE(list, n)
}
```

(C)
```
replace_even(n, list)
{
  x ← list[n]+1
  INSERT(list, n, x)
  REMOVE(list, n)
}
```

(D)
```
replace_even(n, list)
{
  x ← list[n]+1
  REMOVE(list, n)
  INSERT(list, n, x)
}
```

51. A game designer is creating a background image, and wants to include a staircase. Consider the following code, assuming procedures work as they are named:

```
PROCEDURE drawStairs()
{
    draw3by2Box()
    move3UnitsRight()
    draw3by4Box()
    move3UnitsRight()
    draw3by6Box()
    move3UnitsRight()
}
```

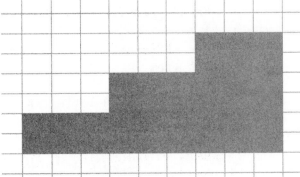

In order to draw three stairs next to each other, individual procedures are made to draw each step, and another method to move three units to the right.

Which of the following procedures below, assuming procedures work as named, would be a valid replacement for the above code?

I.
```
PROCEDURE drawStairs()
{
    drawBox(3,2)
    move3UnitsRight()
    drawBox(3,4)
    move3UnitsRight()
    drawBox(3,6)
    move3UnitsRight()
}
```

II.
```
PROCEDURE drawStairs()
{
    drawBoxAndMoveRight(3,2,3)
    drawBoxAndMoveRight(3,4,3)
    DrawBoxAndMoveRight(3,6,3)
}
```

III.
```
PROCEDURE drawStairs()
{
    n ← 2
    REPEAT UNTL (n > 6)
    {
        drawBoxAndMoveRight3(3,n)
        n ← n + 2
    }
}
```

(A) I only
(B) II only
(C) II and III
(D) I, II, and III

52. Consider the following procedure called mystery (list).

```
PROCEDURE mystery (list)
{
  FOR EACH item IN list
  {
    IF (item ≠ 'a' AND item ≠ 'e' AND item ≠ 'i' AND
    item ≠ 'o' AND item ≠ 'u')
     {
      FOR EACH letter IN list
       {
        DISPLAY (letter)
       }
       DISPLAY " "
     }
  }
}
```

If list CSList contains the following data: ['c', 'o', 'm', 'p', 'u', 't', 'e', 'r'], what will be displayed by mystery (CSList) ?
(A) cmptr cmptr cmptr cmptr cmptr
(B) computer computer computer computer computer
(C) cmptr cmptr cmptr
(D) computer computer computer

53. Monica is surfing the web one day after class. She types the following web address, widgets.cs.fbhs.org, into the URL bar in her browser. Which of the following events is most likely to take place among the DNS servers?
(A) The .org name server will send the IP address of widgets.cs.fbhs.org
(B) The widgets name server will send the IP address of the widgets.cs name server.
(C) The widgets.cs.fbhs.org name server will send the IP address of widgets.cs.fbhs.org
(D) The .org name server will send the IP address of the fbhs.org name server.

54. Without protocols the information sent and received through the Internet would never reach its intended target and even if it did, the message would be a jumbled mess. Review the lists below and select the one that correctly lists each protocol with its function.
(A) TCP/IP identifies the resource requested
    DNS uses a "handshake" to relay packet information
    HTTP translates the name of a web server to a valid IP address
(B) DNS identifies the resource requested
    HTTP uses a "handshake" to relay packet information
    TCP/IP translates the name of a web server to a valid IP address
(C) TCP/IP identifies the resource requested
    HTTP uses a "handshake" to relay packet information
    DNS translates the name of a web server to a valid IP address
(D) HTTP identifies the resource requested
    TCP/IP uses a "handshake" to relay packet information
    DNS translates the name of a web server to a valid IP address

55. You are trying to explain to a group of middle school students how IP addressing works and how the Internet knows where to send things and how to connect. You also want to describe how the addressing system allows for new computers to be added from locations already on the Internet. You have tried to explain the IPv4 addressing system and your only feedback has been blank stares. Which of the following examples accurately describe how the IP addressing and DNS systems direct Internet traffic? Select two answers.

    (A) You explain to the students that US mail uses a system very similar to IPv4 when distributing the mail. You tell them that five digit US zip code is structured like so: the first digit indicates the section of the country, the second digit identifies a specific area within that region, the third number identifies more precise information like a city, the last 2 digits are at the bottom level and are used to represent the most precise information like an area within the city. As cities grow, new locator numbers can be added to define those areas.

    (B) You explain that a school interoffice mail delivery system is similar to the IP addressing system. A person uses an interoffice envelope and puts the recipient's name and location within the district on the front. That envelope is then placed in an outgoing box where it is picked up and taken to a central processing area. From that area, an employee picks up the envelope, reads the address and then delivers it to the person it is addressed to. As new employees are added or removed, the central processing area, simply adds or deletes names from its directory.

    (C) You explain to the students that phone numbers are a form of addressing similar to IP addresses. The area code is the top level and identifies a large area with a group of phone numbers (e.g., a city or region), this is further specified by the three digit prefix which identifies a smaller section (e.g., a community within the city), which is even further specified by the last four digits of the phone number which is assigned to a specific location (e.g., a residence or person). As new people need phone numbers for specific areas, they are assigned a unique four digit code that when added to the other six digits becomes their phone number.

    (D) You explain that the IP and DNS systems are similar to an automotive assembly line. At the top level is the start of the line where the assembly begins on the chassis. As the chassis moves down the line it goes through the various levels of getting more information (parts) added to it. Each part that is added to the chassis represents a lower, more specific level of use (e.g., door, arm rest on door, button on arm rest, etc.). If changes needs to be made or parts added, new steps are added into the assembly process.

56. Bill receives an unsolicited e-mail from an address that appears to be his bank. The e-mail is asking Bill to verify his account information in a reply. The e-mail looks legitimate and even has his bank's logo and address. Bill replies to the email with his account number and security information. The next day, Bill receives a call from his bank that his account has been closed and all of the funds have been withdrawn. Bill has been defrauded and is a victim of which e-mail scam?
    (A) Spearing
    (B) Social Engineering
    (C) Phishing
    (D) Denial of Service

57. Use the diagram below to answer the following question.

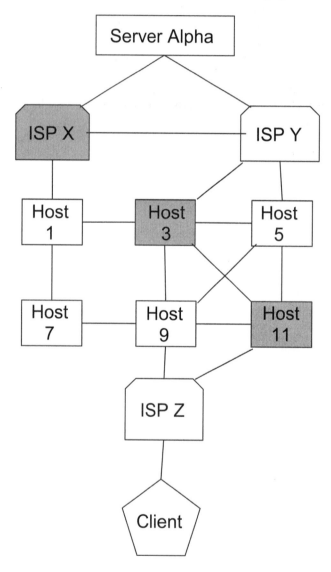

If the client requests data from Server Alpha, which of the statements below BEST describes what will happen if ISP X, Host 3, and Host 11 are not working?
(A) The Client will not receive any data due to the outage
(B) ISP Y will receive packets indicating a failure to Host 3 and re-route the data to a working host
(C) Host 1 will compensate for the outage and route the data accordingly
(D) Host 7 will notify both the client and Server Alpha which nodes are not functioning.

58. When the DNS system was first created there was no reason to consider security being built into it as all it did was convert plain text host names into IP addresses. However, as technology has evolved and cyber threats have increased, the DNS has come under attack because of its poor security. One of the biggest concerns with DNS security is cache poisoning. DNS servers sometimes don't have an answer to a request in their cache and they pass the query off to another DNS server. If that server has incorrect information, a poisoning of the DNS can occur. Which of the following correctly identify methods of DNS cache poisoning? Select two answers.
(A) Masquerading
(B) DNS Key Distribution
(C) DNS BINDing
(D) Rogue Servers

59. Consider the two cryptography representations below when answering the question.

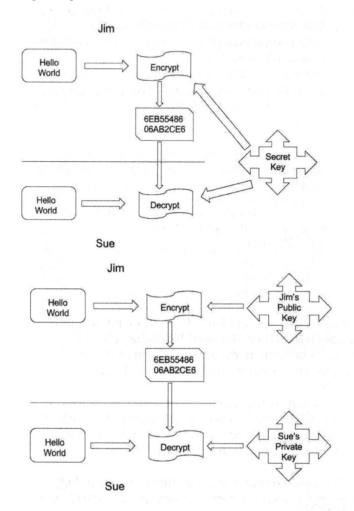

These drawings depict two fundamental cryptographic concepts. Which of the choices below properly identify these concepts?
(A) Symmetric and Steganography
(B) Hash Codes and Key Transfers
(C) Lexicographic and Asymmetric
(D) Asymmetric and Symmetric

60. Maddie has purchased a video from a video website and wants to download it to her laptop. Her current connection speed is 700 kilobytes per second (kps). Approximately how long will the download take if her video is 400 megabytes in size?
(A) 57.1 seconds
(B) 571 seconds
(C) 175 seconds
(D) 1.75 seconds

61. Noah has just purchased a new laptop and a new wireless router for his apartment. Which of the following precautions will ensure that the other residents in the apartment complex will not be able to see Noah's wireless network?
    I. Disabling the SSID broadcasting
    II. Ensure that encryption is enabled
    III. Enable MAC filtering
    IV. Resetting the router security settings to prevent unauthorized access

    (A) I
    (B) II and IV
    (C) II, III, and IV
    (D) All of the above

62. Which of the following protocol standardization is NOT a function of the IETF (Internet Engineering Task Force)?
    (A) Hypertext Transfer Protocol
    (B) Internet Protocol
    (C) JavaScript Coding Protocol
    (D) Simple Mail Transfer Protocol

63. With rapid growth in the demand for information, entertainment, and other web-based activities, the need for stable, always available servers has become paramount. Which of the examples below does not indicate a system that has been built on a distributive model?
    (A) A MMORPG site builds multiple server farms to ensure that the game is always active and has no, to very minimal downtime.
    (B) A film company that makes animated short films designs and builds a render farm to assist in the processing of their animations.
    (C) A web development company decides that in order to help their employees collaborate, have better version control, and be more efficient, they are going to create a version control system for their employees to use for their projects.
    (D) A company decides to incorporate a backup system for all of its computers. It purchases stand alone, backup drives and installs them on each machine in the business to ensure that work files are not lost.

64. In the United States many communities have CCTV, traffic, and other surveillance cameras to ensure the safety of the people. These systems allow the various governments to gather a lot of data on it citizenry. Which of the statements below is the most reasonable argument against the amount of surveillance that is being done?
    (A) Legal regulations and policies regarding the use of video footage dramatically lags behind the technology that is making increased surveillance possible.
    (B) The amount of video surveillance is driving crime deeper underground and making it harder for law enforcement to catch criminals.
    (C) The amount of video surveillance equipment is causing undue burdens on the finances of the communities where they are located. The cost of maintenance alone is not worth the "safety" that is provided.
    (D) Mistrust of government agencies is increasing due to the perceived "spying" of the government on its population. Citizens are not seeing a positive enough return on the investment to outweigh the loss of their privacy.

65. With the popularity of digital editing tools for music, video, and text, it has become increasingly more likely that some individuals will use the technology in ways that may violate copyright laws, even if it's unknowingly. Which of the scenarios below are most likely to be actual copyright violations? Select two answers.
    (A) McKenzie is creating a video project for her U.S. History class. For her project she has collected several clips from various movies depicting wars that the U.S. has fought. She provides a brief commentary on each clip and then shows the clip before moving on. She uploads her project to a popular video sharing site so her teacher can view it.
    (B) Robert dreams of being a musician. He has purchased top-of-the-line sound editing software for his new laptop. Robert begins creating music using the prebuilt loops and sounds that come with the software. For one piece, Robert copies sixteen bars of instrumental music from a popular pop song. It flows nicely with his original music and he sells the new song though a music site for indie recording artists.
    (C) Steven is an avid movie watcher and buys lots of DVDs. He has purchased software that allows him to make copies of his DVDs. He stores the copies in his closet and has occasionally had to use one when friends come over and he can't locate the original.
    (D) Emily is an engineering student at a major university. She has discovered that the CAD software her professors are using is available free to students online through the manufacturer's website. Emily goes to the website and downloads the very large file and makes multiple copies on data CDs for the rest of her class. She distributes these disks at the next class meeting.

66. Digital content is created everyday by both professionals and amateurs. Many of these people would like to share their content with others across the World Wide Web. Creative Commons' licenses allow people to post their digital content online for others to use but still maintain some legal protection of their creations. Which of the licenses listed below is NOT a Creative Commons license?

(A) A license that allows for redistribution, commercial and non-commercial, as long as it is passed along unchanged and in whole, with credit to you.

(B) A license that lets others remix, tweak, and build upon your work non-commercially, as long as they credit you and license their new creations under the identical terms.

(C) A license that only allows others to download your works and share them with others as long as they credit you, but they can't change them in any way or use them commercially. This license is the most restrictive.

(D) A license that lets others distribute and/or sell your work, even commercially, with only credit given to you. With this license you are giving your creation to the public to use as they wish.

67. Ripley is a very active member of her robotics team. As the team captain she is always working not only to help her team get information, but to pass on useful information to other teams in the robotics community. The organization that Ripley's robotics team competes in maintains a site with entries regarding robot building, programming, and other aspects of the competition. One benefit of this site is that its users have the ability to modify and/or edit the informational articles that have been published. The entries are dynamic and ever-changing. Which of the following best describes the type of site that Ripley is using?

(A) RSS Feed
(B) Wiki
(C) Newsgroup
(D) Webopedia

68. The power of computers to enhance scientific methods and increase business performance has grown steadily as the technology has improved. Computational science is a growing field. It allows for enhanced experimenting and results-based research. Review the choices below and select the option that would NOT be a valid application of computational science.
    (A) A group of scientists from NOAA design a Monte Carlo experiment to recreate how tsunamis are impacted by varying atmospheric conditions such as water temperature, wind speed and water current.
    (B) A biologist uses a computer simulation to measure the varying dynamics of predator/prey relationships in the U.S. National Park system. She wants to determine the impact of a particular predator being reintroduced to the park system.
    (C) A chemist is trying to create a new plastic that is less rigid and therefore stronger. He develops a computer program that will allow him to quickly research various chemical properties and compositions that he can utilize in his laboratory experiments.
    (D) A group of paleontologists and geologists are trying to determine how a set of fossils was spread throughout a river basin. They create a program that will model the terrain as they expect it would have looked at the time the fossils were deposited, and the various natural processes that could have led to the fossil bed ending up in its current state.

69. The explosion of the Internet has brought diverse ideas and beliefs to people around the world. However, not all governments are open to their citizenry having access to these new ideologies. China is one of the most well-known censors of the Internet for its population. Review the list below and select the two known forms of censorship currently used in China.
    (A) The Chinese government provides its ISPs with lists of keywords that they use to block access to websites and/or webpages that contain those restricted words.
    (B) The Chinese government embeds cookies on the machines of all Internet users to track the sites that are visited and the search terms that are being used.
    (C) The Chinese government employs hackers to create viruses that are deployed through Chinese ISPs to their users. The viruses are forms of spyware that return not only the web searches of the user but returns a directory of the files the users are creating on their own.
    (D) The Chinese government hires people to post pro-government messages and look for possible efforts to initiate public protests and/or activism.

70. As part of its outreach program, a high school robotics team has decided to offer online programming assistance to other teams across the country. In addition to sharing and demonstrating programming concepts, the team would like to be able to answer questions in real time from other teams across the country. What is the <u>best</u> option for the robotics team to use to achieve its goals?
    (A) Conduct their training sessions via video conference so that teams from across the country engage each other and the host team and receive immediate feedback.
    (B) Post videos showing the programming process to an online video hosting site and provide an e-mail address where viewers can send questions.
    (C) Create a slide presentation that shows a step-by-step process for writing a program.
    (D) Provide finished programming code to anyone who wants it.

71. A problem on many college campuses is the theft of student bicycles. A group of enterprising students has developed a product that can be attached to a bicycle and uses GPS positioning to locate the bike should it be stolen. The students are very technologically savvy but have very little actual business experience. Based on their backgrounds, what is the most likely method the students can use to raise funding for their venture?
    (A) Apply for a small business loan through an online bank.
    (B) Utilize a crowdsourcing website to raise the needed capital.
    (C) Create a bulk email campaign that sends emails to all of the students on their college campus asking for support and funding.
    (D) Design and create a website in hopes a venture capitalist will come to them.

72. A severe weather system is moving through the Gulf Coast of Texas. Emma, a journalism student from the northeast, is visiting her roommate's family and is caught in the storm. She witnesses first-hand the effects of severe flooding and a tornado, and is able to capture video and photos on her cell phone. Emma decides she wants to recount her experiences to people back east who have never experienced such severe weather. What methods could Emma use so that her story, video, and photos will likely be seen by the maximum number of people? Select <u>two</u> answers.
    (A) Posting her article along with the videos and photos to her journalism blog, which has several hundred followers.
    (B) E-mail the local news media back home and offer them her videos and photos.
    (C) Utilize all of her social media sites so that her friends and family can also take part in spreading the information.
    (D) Write an article for an online journal and include several of her photographs.

73. Computing technology makes large contributions to multiple fields outside of the computer industry. Which of the items below is NOT a technology advancement in law enforcement that is being used by officers in the field?
    (A) Facial recognition software that allows officers to instantly run checks on potential suspects.
    (B) Software that allows for predictive policing and a better allocation of police resources.
    (C) Networked police cars that have instant access to information on suspects and are always connected to a central station.
    (D) The use of drones to record and surveil in areas that are too dangerous or too remote for officers.

74. Which of the following scenarios relating to open source software and its licensing are violations and raise ethical/legal issues? Select two answers.
    (A) A developer uses the code in an open source, GPL-licensed (General Public License) web browser to create a derivative product and releases that product without including all of the original code.
    (B) A developer takes the code of an open source e-mail program that has a BSD (Berkeley Software Distribution) license, makes minor changes to the appearance of the interface, and releases it with no attribution and without including the original source code.
    (C) A developer uses a piece of open source code that has a MPL (Mozilla Public License), and combines it with their own proprietary code. That new, combined code is then licensed for commercial use.
    (D) A developer takes code used for an open source, GNU-licensed 3d modeling software; he renames it without changing any of the code and shares it with peers without providing them with the source code he used.

Answers for Multiple-Choice Questions

1. **Answer: C.** The '.' has 6 zeros, all of the other characters have five or fewer.

Learning Objectives	Essential Knowledge
LO 2.1.1 Describe the variety of abstractions used to represent data.	**EK 2.1.1A** Digital data is represented by abstractions at different levels.
	EK 2.1.1B At the lowest level, all digital data are represented by bits.
	EK 2.1.1C At a higher level, bits are grouped to represent abstractions, including but not limited to numbers, characters, and color.
	EK 2.1.1D Number bases, including binary, decimal, and hexadecimal, are used to represent and investigate digital data.
	EK 2.1.1E At one of the lowest levels of abstraction, digital data is represented in binary (base 2) using only combinations of the digits zero and one.
	EK 2.1.1G Numbers can be converted from any base to any other base.

2. **Answer: C.** Octal is base 8, so we can see how many times each power of 8 goes into the differences.

Learning Objectives	Essential Knowledge
LO 2.1.1 Describe the variety of abstractions used to represent data.	**EK 2.1.1C** At a higher level, bits are grouped to represent abstractions, including but not limited to numbers, characters, and color.
	EK 2.1.1G Numbers can be converted from any base to any other base.

3. **Answer: D.** The product will eventually get so large that it will cause an overflow.

Learning Objectives	Essential Knowledge
LO 2.1.2 Explain how binary sequences are used to represent digital data.	**EK 2.1.2B** In many programming languages, the fixed number of bits used to represent characters or integers limits the range of integer values and mathematical operations; this limitation can result in overflow or other errors.
LO 5.5.1 Employ appropriate mathematical and logical concepts in programming.	**EK 5.5.1E** Logical concepts and Boolean algebra are fundamental to programming.

4. **Answer: A**. A is a logic error, where rounding was done at the wrong place.

Learning Objectives	Essential Knowledge
LO 2.1.2 Explain how binary sequences are used to represent digital data.	**EK 2.1.2C** In many programming languages, the fixed number of bits used to represent real numbers (as floating-point numbers) limits the range of floating-point values and mathematical operations; this limitation can result in round off and other errors.

5. **Answer: D**. Operating systems build on programming languages, which build on machine language, which build on binary, which builds on gates.

Learning Objectives	Essential Knowledge
LO 2.2.3 Identify multiple levels of abstractions that are used when writing programs.	**EK 2.2.3D** In an abstraction hierarchy, higher levels of abstraction (the most general concepts) would be placed toward the top and lower-level abstractions (the more specific concepts) toward the bottom.
	EK 2.2.3E Binary data is processed by physical layers of computing hardware, including gates, chips, and components.
	EK 2.2.3F A logic gate is a hardware abstraction that is modeled by a Boolean function.

6. **Answers: A, D**. High level programs focus on problem-solving strategies rather than machine level instructions, and they allow for code re-use with , for example, variables and procedures.

Learning Objectives	Essential Knowledge
LO 2.2.3 Identify multiple levels of abstractions that are used when writing programs.	**EK 2.2.3A** Different programming languages offer different levels of abstraction.
	EK 2.2.3B High-level programming languages provide more abstractions for the programmer and make it easier for people to read and write a program.
	EK 2.2.3C Code in a programming language is often translated into code in another (lower-level) language to be executed on a computer.

7. **Answer: C.** Hardware can be low-level or high-level.

Learning Objectives	Essential Knowledge
LO 2.2.3 Identify multiple levels of abstractions that are used when writing programs.	EK 2.2.3E Binary data is processed by physical layers of computing hardware, including gates, chips, and components. EK 2.2.3F A logic gate is a hardware abstraction that is modeled by a Boolean function. EK 2.2.3H A hardware component can be low-level like a transistor or high-level like a video card.

8. **Answers: A, B.** Both set the count equal to 0 before entering the loop, then compare two random numbers from intervals of size 2.

Learning Objectives	Essential Knowledge
LO 2.3.1 Use models and simulations to represent phenomena.	EK 2.3.1A Models and simulations are simplified representations of more complex objects or phenomena. EK 2.3.1B Models may use different abstractions or levels of abstraction depending on the objects or phenomena being posed.
LO 5.2.1 Explain how programs implement algorithms.	EK 5.2.1B Program instructions are executed sequentially. EK 5.2.1C Program instructions may involve variables that are initialized and updated, read, and written.

9. **Answer: D.** The procedure removes and displays all multiples of 3.

Learning Objectives	Essential Knowledge
LO 5.3.1 Use abstraction to manage complexity in programs.	EK 5.3.1A Procedures are reusable programming abstractions. EK 5.3.1B A procedure is a named grouping of programming instructions. EK 5.3.1G Parameters provide different values as input to procedures when they are called in a program. EK 5.3.1K List and list operations, such as add, remove, and search, are common in many programs.

10. **Answer: C.** cube (2) is 2 * 2 * 2, which is 8. cube(8) is 8 * 8 * 8, which is 512.

Learning Objectives	Essential Knowledge
LO 5.3.1 Use abstraction to manage complexity in programs.	EK 5.3.1C Procedures reduce the complexity of writing and maintaining programs.

11. **Answer: B.** x changes to 2, y remains the same, so the product of x and y (2 and 2) is 4.

Learning Objectives	Essential Knowledge
LO 5.3.1 Use abstraction to manage complexity in programs.	**EK 5.3.1D** Procedures have names and may have parameters and return values.
LO 5.5.1 Employ appropriate mathematical and logical concepts in programming.	**EK 5.5.1A** Numbers and numerical concepts are fundamental to programming. **EK 5.5.1D** Mathematical expressions using arithmetic operators are part of most programming languages.

12. **Answer: C.** Antler size is most likely extraneous information, given the description in the question.

Learning Objectives	Essential Knowledge
LO 2.3.1 Use models and simulations to represent phenomena.	**EK 2.3.1C** Models often omit unnecessary features of the objects or phenomena that are being modeled. **EK 2.3.1D** Simulations mimic real-world events without the cost or danger of building and testing phenomena in the real world.
LO 5.4.1 Evaluate the correctness of a program.	**EK 5.4.1F** Knowledge of what a program is supposed to do is required in order to find most program errors. **EK 5.4.1G** Examples of intended behavior on specific inputs help people understand what a program is supposed to do.

13. **Answer: C.** The simulation always chooses 1 of 52 cards, so the card must be returned each time.

Learning Objectives	Essential Knowledge
LO 2.3.1 Use models and simulations to represent phenomena.	**EK 2.3.1A** Models and simulations are simplified representations of more complex objects or phenomena. **EK 2.3.1B** Models may use different abstractions or levels of abstraction depending on the objects or phenomena being posed.

14. **Answer: D**. All of the above are possible outcomes.

Learning Objectives	Essential Knowledge
LO 2.3.2 Use models and simulations to formulate, refine, and test hypotheses.	EK 2.3.2A Models and simulations facilitate the formulation and refinement of hypotheses related to the objects or phenomena under consideration. EK 2.3.2B Hypotheses are formulated to explain the objects or phenomena being modeled. EK 2.3.2C Hypotheses are refined by examining that insights that models and simulations provide into the objects or phenomena. EK 2.3.2D The results of simulations may generate new knowledge and new hypotheses related to the phenomena being modeled. EK 2.3.2F Simulations can facilitate extensive and rapid testing of models. EK 2.3.2H Rapid and extensive testing allows models to be changed to accurately reflect the objects or phenomena being modeled.

15. **Answer: A**. While the other options all include fields that need to participate, they also leave out at least one important field in each case.

Learning Objectives	Essential Knowledge
LO 3.1.2 Collaborate when processing information to gain insight and knowledge.	EK 3.1.2B Collaboration facilitates solving computational problems by applying multiple perspectives, experiences, and skill sets.

16. **Answer: C**. Effective collaboration teams will produce all of the correct answers, and an effective leader should play to the strengths of his/her team rather than try to get members to think the same way.

Learning Objectives	Essential Knowledge
LO 3.1.2 Collaborate when processing information to gain insight and knowledge.	EK 3.1.2E Collaborating face-to-face and using online collaborative tools can facilitate processing information to gain insight and knowledge.

17. **Answers: C, D**. The very nature of large data sets is what makes them desirable for scientists. It is their size that makes collaboration necessary and to limit the amount of data a collaborative group works with would be counterproductive.

Learning Objectives	Essential Knowledge
LO 3.1.2 Collaborate when processing information to gain insight and knowledge.	EK 3.1.2F Investigating large data sets collaboratively can lead to insight and knowledge not obtained when working alone.

18. **Answer: C**. Either algorithm will work. The only difference between the two is the order in which you do the sorts and the counts.

Learning Objectives	Essential Knowledge
LO 3.2.1 Extract information from data to discover and explain connections or trends.	EK 3.2.1B Large data sets provide opportunities for identifying trends, making connections in data, and solving problems.

19. **Answers: A, C**. These exclusion searches will omit the word at the end from the returned search results.

Learning Objectives	Essential Knowledge
LO 3.2.1 Extract information from data to discover and explain connections or trends.	EK 3.2.1D Search tools are essential for efficiently finding information.

20. **Answer: D**. Recommender systems for movies, music, news, etc. are all examples of information filtering systems. An information filtering system removes redundant or unwanted information from an information stream before presenting it to a human user.

Learning Objectives	Essential Knowledge
LO 3.2.1 Extract information from data to discover and explain connections or trends.	EK 3.2.1E Information filtering systems are important tools for finding information and recognizing patterns in the information.

21. **Answer: C**. It is often not practical or feasible to grant access of data to just one person in an organization.

Learning Objectives	Essential Knowledge
LO 3.2.2 Determine how large data sets impact the use of computational processes to discover information and knowledge.	EK 3.2.2D Maintaining privacy of large data sets containing personal information can be challenging.

22. **Answers: A, C.** Cloud storage is not guaranteed to be secure, and a government employee should use the resources provided to him. A password should never be shared. Following typical company "best practices" an IT technician would normally make a request for individual user information in person.

Learning Objectives	Essential Knowledge
LO 3.3.1 Analyze how data representation, storage, security, and transmission of data involve computational manipulation of information.	**EK 3.3.1A** Digital data representations involve trade-offs related to storage, security, and privacy concerns. **EK 3.3.1B** Security concerns engender trade-offs in storing and transmitting information.

23. **Answer: B.** Because lossy formats lose data by the nature of their compression, this statement is false.

Learning Objectives	Essential Knowledge
LO 3.3.1 Analyze how data representation, storage, security, and transmission of data involve computational manipulation of information.	**EK 3.3.1C** There are trade-offs is using lossy and lossless compression techniques for storing and transmitting data.

24. **Answer: C.** All statements are true except III. Manual creation of metadata includes information beyond file size, data types, etc., and it is not inherently less accurate than automatically generated metadata.

Learning Objectives	Essential Knowledge
LO 3.2.1 Extract information from data to discover and explain connections or trends.	**EK 3.2.1G** Metadata is data about data. **EK 3.2.1I** Metadata can increase the effective use of data or data sets by providing additional information about various aspects of that data.

25. **Answer: C.** Cloud-based storage services provide access to data from multiple locations at the same time. Although a Mainframe Computer can also be accessed from multiple locations, it often requires special software installation on machines and is not "easy" to new users.

Learning Objectives	Essential Knowledge
LO 3.3.1 Analyze how data representation, storage, security, and transmission of data involve computational manipulation of information.	**EK 3.3.1H** The choice of storage media affects both the methods and costs of manipulating the data it contains.

26. **Answer: C**. Both algorithms filter the data, then count some of the remaining data based on a true or false condition.

Learning Objectives	Essential Knowledge
LO 4.1.1 Develop an algorithm for implementation in a program.	EK 4.1.1A Sequencing, selection, and iteration are building blocks of algorithms.
	EK 4.1.1I Developing a new algorithm to solve a problem can yield insight into the problem.
LO 5.1.2 Develop a correct program to solve problems.	EK 5.1.2A An iterative process of program development helps in developing a correct program to solve problems.

27. **Answer: D**. Algorithm D gathers data, sums up the data, looks at options, then selects the best option.

Learning Objectives	Essential Knowledge
LO 4.1.1 Develop an algorithm for implementation in a program.	EK 4.1.1B Sequencing is the application of each step of an algorithm in the order in which the statements are given.

28. **Answer: A**. The GIF uses less memory. Though more complex, it is more efficient.

Learning Objectives	Essential Knowledge
LO 3.3.1 Analyze how data representation, storage, security, and transmission of data involve computational manipulation of information.	EK 3.3.1D Lossless data compression reduces the number of bits stored or transmitted but allows complete reconstruction of the original data.
	EK 3.3.1E Lossy data compression can significantly reduce the number of bits stored or transmitted at the cost of being able to reconstruct only an approximation of the original data.
LO 4.2.4 Evaluate algorithms analytically and empirically for efficiency, correctness, and clarity.	EK 4.2.4E Sometimes, more efficient algorithms are more complex.
	EK 4.2.4G Efficiency includes both execution time and memory usage.

29. **Answers: A, B**. Choice A involves starting with a smaller problem to solve larger instances, and Choice B involves working with known algorithms.

Learning Objectives	Essential Knowledge
LO 4.2.4 Evaluate algorithms analytically and empirically for efficiency, correctness, and clarity.	EK 4.2.4F Finding an efficient algorithm for a problem can help solve larger instances of the problem.

30. **Answer: A.** Efficiency includes both execution time and memory usage.

Learning Objectives	Essential Knowledge
LO 4.2.4 Evaluate algorithms analytically and empirically for efficiency, correctness, and clarity.	EK 4.2.4G Efficiency includes both execution time and memory usage.

31. **Answer: B.** Although the sort is an unnecessary step, Algorithm II will search each element on the list to find the correct entries. Algorithm I attempts to perform a binary search on unsorted data.

Learning Objectives	Essential Knowledge
LO 4.2.4 Evaluate algorithms analytically and empirically for efficiency, correctness, and clarity.	EK 4.2.4H Linear search can be used when searching for an item in any list; binary search can be used only when the list is sorted.

32. **Answers: A, B.** Both are excellent reasons to use a statically typed language. Choice A results in more efficient code, and Choice B results in cleaner code.

Learning Objectives	Essential Knowledge
LO 4.1.2 Express an algorithm in a language.	EK 4.1.2D Different languages are better suited for expressing different algorithms.
	EK 4.1.2E Some programming languages are designed for specific domains and are better for expressing algorithms in those domains.

33. **Answers: A, B.** Both choices assign values to the number cubes, then calculate the sum, then display the correct output.

Learning Objectives	Essential Knowledge
LO 4.1.1 Develop an algorithm for implementation in a program.	EK 4.1.1A Sequencing, selection, and iteration are building blocks of algorithms.
LO 4.1.2 Express an algorithm in a language.	EK 4.1.2B Natural language and pseudocode describe algorithms so that humans can understand them.

34. **Answer: A.** More input will increase the number of iterations required to solve the problem.

Learning Objectives	Essential Knowledge
LO 4.2.1 Explain the difference between algorithms that run in a reasonable time and those that do not run in a reasonable time.	**EK 4.2.1A** Many problems can be solved in a reasonable time. **EK 4.2.1B** Reasonable time means that the number of steps the algorithm takes is less than or equal to a polynomial function (constant, linear, square, cube, etc.) of the size of the input.
LO 4.2.4 Evaluate algorithms analytically and empirically for efficiency, correctness, and clarity.	**EK 4.2.4H** Linear search can be used when searching for an item in any list; binary search can be used only when the list is sorted.

35. **Answer: A.** Heuristic approaches can be used to find a solution that works well enough to get the job done.

Learning Objectives	Essential Knowledge
LO 4.2.1 Explain the difference between algorithms that run in a reasonable time and those that do not run in a reasonable time.	**EK 4.2.1C** Some problems cannot be solved in a reasonable time, even for small input sizes. **EK 4.2.1D** Some problems can be solved but not in a reasonable time. In these cases, heuristic approaches may be helpful to find solutions in reasonable time.

36. **Answers: B, D.** Choice B is true because you cannot guarantee that a certain algorithm is the best; you can only be assured that it works. Choice D is true, as image compression is an important part of computing.

Learning Objectives	Essential Knowledge
LO 4.2.2 Explain the difference between solvable and unsolvable problems in computer science.	**EK 4.2.2A** A heuristic is a technique that may allow us to find an approximate solution when typical methods fail to find an exact solution.

37. **Answer: B.** The robot moves forward as long as there is an open space ahead to get to the right, then moves down to the bottom, and rotates to face east.

Learning Objectives	Essential Knowledge
LO. 4.1.1 Develop an algorithm for implementation in a program.	**EK 4.1.1A** Sequencing, selection, and iteration are building blocks of algorithms.
LO 4.1.2 Express an algorithm in a language.	**EK 4.1.2I** Clarity and readability are important considerations when expressing an algorithm in a language.

38. **Answers: A, D.** Choice A uses a list instruction to add each value in the list, then divides that sum by the number of items in the list. Choice D uses a REPEAT loop to do the same thing.

Learning Objectives	Essential Knowledge
LO 5.1.1 Develop a program for creative expression, to satisfy personal curiosity, or to create new knowledge.	**EK 5.1.1A** Programs are developed and used in a variety of ways by a wide range of people depending on the goals of the programmer.
LO 5.5.1 Employ appropriate mathematical and logical concepts in programming.	**EK 5.5.1A** Numbers and numerical concepts are fundamental to programming.

39. **Answer: B.** Once the values become higher than the maximum allowable values, problems in the output will occur.

Learning Objectives	Essential Knowledge
LO 5.5.1 Employ appropriate mathematical and logical concepts in programming.	**EK 5.5.1B** Integers may be constrained in the maximum and minimum vales that can be represented in a program because of storage limitations.

40. **Answer: C.** The computer is incapable of using pi and finding an answer with infinite precision. The landscaper should find an approximation that works for him.

Learning Objectives	Essential Knowledge
LO 5.5.1 Employ appropriate mathematical and logical concepts in programming.	**EK 5.5.1C** Real numbers are approximated by floating-point representations that do not necessarily have infinite precision.

41. **Answer: B.** Choice B checks to see if each number is odd by finding the modulus, then adds the number to the sum if it is.

Learning Objectives	Essential Knowledge
LO 5.1.2 Develop a correct program to solve problems.	**EK 5.1.2B** Developing correct program components and then combining them helps in creating correct programs.
LO 5.2.1 Explain how programs implement algorithms.	**EK 5.2.1B** Program instructions are executed sequentially.
LO 5.5.1 Employ appropriate mathematical and logical concepts in programming.	**EK 5.5.1D** Mathematical expressions using arithmetic operators are part of most programming languages.

42. **Answer: B**. The value of x is increased by 1 if it is greater than 5. Either way, x is decreased by 1 after the if statement is evaluated and the appropriate code is executed.

Learning Objectives	Essential Knowledge
LO 5.5.1 Employ appropriate mathematical and logical concepts in programming.	**EK 5.5.1E** Logical concepts and Boolean algebra are fundamental to programming. **EK 5.5.1G** Intuitive and formal reasoning about program components using Boolean concepts helps in developing correct programs.

43. **Answer: D**. The initial "OR" condition is met, and so is the "AND" condition that follows. x is assigned y's value, which is 20. y is assigned x's value, which is now 20. Both x and y are doubled.

Learning Objectives	Essential Knowledge
LO 5.5.1 Employ appropriate mathematical and logical concepts in programming.	**EK 5.5.1E** Logical concepts and Boolean algebra are fundamental to programming. **EK 5.5.1F** Compound expressions using *and, or,* and *not* are part of most programming languages. **EK 5.5.1G** Intuitive and formal reasoning about program components using Boolean concepts helps in developing correct programs.

44. **Answer: C**. The procedure returns a true if and only if the robot cannot move in any direction.

Learning Objectives	Essential Knowledge
LO 5.4.1 Evaluate the correctness of a program.	**EK 5.4.1C** Meaningful names for variables and procedures help people better understand programs.
LO 5.5.1 Employ appropriate mathematical and logical concepts in programming.	**EK 5.5.1E** Logical concepts and Boolean algebra are fundamental to programming.

45. **Answer: D**. We do not know what the code is trying to achieve.

Learning Objectives	Essential Knowledge
LO 5.4.1 Evaluate the correctness of a program.	**EK 5.4.1E** Locating and correcting errors in a program is called debugging a program. **EK 5.4.1F** Knowledge of what a program is supposed to do is required in order to find most program errors.

46. **Answer: A**. The robot should not be blocked on the right, in order to turn. At the end, the robot will be facing west, but the objective will be met.

Learning Objectives	Essential Knowledge
LO 5.5.1 Employ appropriate mathematical and logical concepts in programming.	EK 5.5.1G Intuitive and formal reasoning about program components using Boolean concepts helps in developing correct programs.

47. **Answer: D**. North is not an acceptable direction in the CSP reference.

Learning Objectives	Essential Knowledge
LO 5.3.1 Use abstraction to manage complexity in programs.	EK 5.3.1D Procedures have names and may have parameters and return values. EK 5.3.1G Parameters provide different values as input to procedures when they are called in a program. EK 5.3.1M Application program interfaces (APIs) and libraries simplify complex programming tasks. EK 5.3.1N Documentation for an API/library is an important aspect of programming. EK 5.3.1O APIs connect software components, allowing them to communicate.

48. **Answer: B**. Choice B repeats the process, selecting one operation for n, and displaying the value.

Learning Objectives	Essential Knowledge
LO 5.2.1 Explain how programs implement algorithms.	EK 5.2.1A Algorithms are implemented using program instructions that are processed during program execution.

49. **Answer: A**. The code must include a selector to determine if the ticket is for a senior or a non-senior.

Learning Objectives	Essential Knowledge
LO 5.5.1 Employ appropriate mathematical and logical concepts in programming.	EK 5.5.1E Logical concepts and Boolean algebra are fundamental to programming.

50. **Answer: D**. The original item is removed, and then replaced by the new value, ensuring that the correct value is inserted and all other values and indices remain the same.

Learning Objectives	Essential Knowledge
LO 5.3.1 Use abstraction to manage complexity in programs.	EK 5.3.1A Procedures are reusable programming abstractions. EK 5.3.1B A procedure is a named grouping of programming instructions. EK 5.3.1G Parameters provide different values as input to procedures when they are called in a program. EK 5.3.1K Lists and list operations, such as add, remove, and search, are common in many programs.

51. **Answer: D**. All of the above options simplify the original code. The first creates a box given the base and height and a separate call to move 3 right, the second takes in a base, height, and amount to move right, and the last take a base and a height.

Learning Objectives	Essential Knowledge
LO 2.2.1 Develop an abstraction when writing a program or creating other computational artifacts.	EK 2.2.1A The process of developing an abstraction involves removing detail and generalizing functionality. EK 2.2.1B An abstraction extracts common features from specific examples in order to generalize concepts. EK 2.2.1C An abstraction generalizes functionality with input parameters that allow software reuse.

52. **Answer: B**. If the list item is not a vowel, the procedure displays the entire contents of the list, plus a space.

Learning Objectives	Essential Knowledge
LO 5.3.1 Use abstraction to manage complexity in programs.	EK 5.3.1A Procedures are reusable programming abstractions. EK 5.3.1B A procedure is a named grouping of programming instructions. EK 5.3.1G Parameters provide different values as input to procedures when they are called in a program. EK 5.3.1I Strings and string operations, including concatenation and some form of substring, are common in many programs. EK 5.3.1K Lists and list operations, such as add, remove, and search, are common in many programs.

53. **Answer: C.** Because of the hierarchy that is inherent in the structure of the domain name system (DNS) servers and because each uniform resource locator (URL) requires a specific Internet protocol (IP) address, the name server requires the complete address to obtain the desired IP.

Learning Objectives	Essential Knowledge
LO 6.1.1 Explain the abstractions in the Internet and how the Internet functions.	**EK 6.1.1G** The domain name system (DNS) translates domain names to IP addresses.

54. **Answer: D.** The Internet requires multiple protocols in order to function properly. Hypertext Transfer Protocol (HTTP) is what allows us to see text displayed on our browser. It passes the text structure from one part of the web to another. Transmission Control Protocol / Internet Protocol (TCP/IP) is the communication language that allows data to be sent over the Internet. TCP breaks the data down into smaller sections called packets. It also reassembles them. IP deals with the addressing and sending and receiving of those packets.

Learning Objectives	Essential Knowledge
LO 6.1.1 Explain the abstractions in the Internet and how the Internet functions.	**EK 6.1.1C** Devices and networks that make up the Internet are connected and communicate using addresses and protocols.
LO 6.2.2 Explain how the characteristics of the Internet influence the systems built on it.	**EK 6.2.2G** Standards for packets and routing included transmission control protocol/Internet protocol (TCP/IP).
	EK 6.2.2H Standards for sharing information and communicating between browsers and servers on the Web include HTTP and secure sockets layer/transport layer security (SSL/TLS).

55. **Answers: A, C.** With more than four billion potential 32-bit IP addresses, Internet routers could not realistically maintain table entries for each one. Routers must be capable of delivering data to any of those addresses. Their *routing tables* must, at the least, be able to indicate the next step in the delivery process for each address. The solution to this dilemma is to design the tables so that one entry can match multiple addresses. The most common way to achieve this is to assign addresses in a hierarchical fashion, so that addresses physically close together share a common address prefix. What is unique about IP addresses is their use of a binary, rather than a decimal hierarchy. In addition, in order for the DNS system to find the addresses it is looking for, the addressing must be scalable. Ans. B is incorrect because the method of addressing and routing the interoffice mail is not done in the same method as IP; this example uses flat addressing and hierarchical addressing. Ans. D is wrong for much the same reason except that on an assembly line there is no addressing used. The products simply move from place to place in a specified order.

Learning Objectives	Essential Knowledge
LO 6.2.1 Explain characteristics of the Internet and the systems built on it.	EK 6.2.1C IP addresses are hierarchical.
LO 6.2.2 Explain how the characteristics of the Internet influence the systems built on it.	EK 6.2.2C Hierarchy in the DNS helps that system scale.

56. **Answer: C.** While social engineering and denial of service are also Internet related frauds, phishing is specific to e-mail fraud.

Learning Objectives	Essential Knowledge
LO 6.3.1 Identify existing cybersecurity concerns and potential options to address these issues with the Internet and the systems built on it.	EK 6.3.1F Phishing, viruses, and other attacks have human and software components.

57. **Answer: B.** Due to the structure of this network, there are working connections which will allow the data requested to be received by the client.

Learning Objectives	Essential Knowledge
LO 6.2.1 Explain characteristics of the Internet and the systems built on it.	EK 6.2.1A The Internet and the systems built on it are hierarchical and redundant. EK 6.2.1B The domain name syntax is hierarchical.
LO 6.2.2 Explain how the characteristics of the Internet influence the systems built on it.	EK 6.2.2A Hierarchy and redundancy help systems scale. EK 6.2.2B The redundancy of routing (i.e., more than one way to route data) between two points on the Internet increases the reliability of the Internet and helps it scale to more devices and more people.

58. **Answers: A, D**. There are several methods of taking advantage of cache poisoning. Two of the most prevalent are masquerading and rogue servers. Masquerading is when information is re-routed to a server pretending to be a trusted source. An attacker can add information to, delete information from, or use the access to embed malware into information going back to the requesting system. Rogue servers are a danger because the information they contain, while not necessarily intentionally bad, may not be trustworthy.

Learning Objectives	Essential Knowledge
LO 6.3.1 Identify existing cybersecurity concerns and potential options to address these issues with the Internet and the systems built on it.	**EK 6.3.1B** The DNS was not designed to be completely secure.
LO 7.1.1 Explain how computing innovations affect communication, interaction, and cognition.	**EK 7.1.1M** The Internet and the Web have enhanced methods of and opportunities for communication and collaboration.

59. **Answer: D**. Symmetric key cryptography utilizes one key for both the sender and receiver of the information (left drawing). Asymmetric key cryptography (public key) utilizes two different but mathematically related keys; a publicly available key encrypts the message but only the receiver's private key can decrypt it.

Learning Objectives	Essential Knowledge
LO 6.3.1 Identify existing cybersecurity concerns and potential options to address these issues with the Internet and the systems built on it.	**EK 6.3.1H** Cryptography is essential to many models of cybersecurity. **EK 6.3.1I** Cryptography has a mathematical foundation. **EK 6.3.1J** Open standards help ensure cryptography is secure.

60. **Answer: B**. There are 1000 kilobytes in a megabyte. Therefore, the file size is 400,000 kilobytes and doing the math (400,000 divided by 700) gives you an answer of 571.

Learning Objectives	Essential Knowledge
LO 6.2.2 Explain how the characteristics of the Internet influence the systems built on it.	**EK 6.2.2F** The Internet is a packet-switched system through which digital data is sent by breaking the data into blocks of bits called packets, which contain both the data being transmitted and control information for routing the data. **6.2.2I** The size and speed of systems affect their use. **6.2.2J** The bandwidth of a system is measure of bit rate – the amount of data (measured in bits) that can be sent in a fixed amount of time.

61. **Answer: A**. While the other options will increase the security of the wireless router, only disabling SSID broadcasting will hide the router from being seen by other computers and/or hand-held scanners.

Learning Objectives	Essential Knowledge
LO 6.3.1 Identify existing cybersecurity concerns and potential options to address these issues with the Internet and the systems built on it.	**EK 6.3.1 A** The trust model of the Internet involves trade-offs. **EK 6.3.1C** Implementing cybersecurity has software, hardware, and human components. **EK 6.3.1G** Antivirus software and firewalls can help prevent unauthorized access to private data.

62. **Answer: C**. The IETF is not responsible for maintaining and updating JavaScript.

Learning Objectives	Essential Knowledge
LO 6.1.1 Explain the abstractions in the Internet and how the Internet functions.	**EK 6.1.1I** Standards such as hypertext transfer protocol (HTTP), Internet Protocol (IP), and simple mail transfer protocol (SMTP) are developed and overseen by the Internet Engineering Task Force (IETF).

63. **Answer: D**. The other three answers are all examples of a distributed system. A distributed system is when the components of a system are all networked together to improve performance, increase "up time", and/or increase efficiency.

Learning Objectives	Essential Knowledge
LO 7.1.2 Explain how people participate in a problem-solving process that scales.	**EK 7.1.2A** Distributed solutions must scale to solve some problems.

64. **Answer: A**. As the technology needed to surveil public areas and as the use of personal surveillance systems increases, the legislative system is lagging behind in keeping up with the creation of policies to monitor and regulate the use of the video obtained from those systems.

Learning Objectives	Essential Knowledge
LO 7.3.1 Analyze the beneficial and harmful effects of computing.	**EK 7.3.1L** Commercial and governmental curation of information may be exploited if privacy and other protections are ignored.

65. **Answers: A, B**. Although students have some leeway with regards to copyright laws and school work, once her project with the copyrighted video clips is posted to a public video sharing site without the permission of the copyright holder, it is a violation. Robert has become one of the many musical artists who have "sampled" another artist's music in their own creations. Unless the original artist is credited and gives permission, sampling is a violation of copyright law.

Learning Objectives	Essential Knowledge
LO 7.3.1 Analyze the beneficial and harmful effects of computing.	EK 7.3.1N Widespread access to digitized information raises questions about intellectual property. EK 7.3.1O Creation of digital audio, video, and textual content by combining existing content has been impacted by copyright concerns.

66. **Answer: D**. Creative Commons is a nonprofit organization that enables the sharing and use of creativity and knowledge through free legal tools.

Learning Objectives	Essential Knowledge
LO 7.2.1 Explain how computing has impacted innovations in other fields.	EK 7.2.1D Open access and Creative Commons have enabled broad access to digital information.

67. **Answer: B**. a wiki is a website that allows collaborative editing of its content and structure by its users.

Learning Objectives	Essential Knowledge
LO 7.1.2 Explain how people participate in a problem-solving process that scales.	EK 7.1.2E Some online services use the contributions of many people to benefit both individuals and society.

68. **Answer: C**. Although the chemist utilizes a computer program he created for his research, the fundamental component of computational science is that the computer model/simulation is what does the experimenting.

Learning Objectives	Essential Knowledge
LO 7.2.1 Explain how computing has impacted innovations in other fields.	EK 7.2.1B Scientific computing has enabled innovation in science and business.

69. **Answers: A, D**. China has admitted that it limits its citizens' access to the World Wide Web. It has admitted that it limits the searches of its people. It is also estimated that China employs around 100,000 people to police the Chinese Internet around the clock.

Learning Objectives	Essential Knowledge
LO 7.3.1 Analyze the beneficial and harmful effects of computing.	EK 7.3.1E Commercial and governmental censorship of digital information raise legal and ethical concerns.

70. **Answer: A.** Since the robotics team's goal is to have a real-time interaction, the only option that allows for this is a video conference.

Learning Objectives	Essential Knowledge
LO 7.1.1 Explain how computing innovations affect communication, interaction, and cognition.	**EK 7.1.1B** Video conferencing and video chat have fostered new ways to communicate and collaborate. **EK 7.1.1 E** Widespread access to information facilitates the identification of problems, development of solutions, and dissemination of results.

71. **Answer: B.** Crowdsourcing has become an excellent way for people with new products but little business background to bring a product to market. Crowdsourcing allows startup businesses to secure funding in the form of small investments from many people rather than trying to secure large investments from only a few people.

Learning Objectives	Essential Knowledge
LO 7.1.2 Explain how people participate in a problem-solving process that scales.	**EK 7.1.2F** Crowdsourcing offers new models for collaboration, such as connecting people with jobs and businesses with funding.

72. **Answers: A, C.** Social media sites and blogs allow individuals to distribute information, images, etc. quickly and efficiently. In addition, by utilizing their followers in disseminating the information, the number of people that have access to the information is increased substantially.

Learning Objectives	Essential Knowledge
LO 7.1.1 Explain how computing innovations affect communication, interaction, and cognition.	**EK 7.1.1C** Social media continues to evolve and fosters new ways to communicate. **EK 7.1.1 H** Social media, such as blogs and Twitter, have enhanced dissemination.

73. **Answer: A.** While facial recognition software is a valid computer technology, the processing is not "instantaneous." Even with networked police cars and access to multiple databases, a facial recognition search takes time.

Learning Objectives	Essential Knowledge
LO 7.2.1 Explain how computing has impacted innovations in other fields.	**EK 7.2.1C** Computing enables innovation by providing the ability to access and share information.

74. **Answers: A, D**. GPL, which is a form of a GNU license, requires that any derivative works (new code or even just a new name) MUST include the original source code that was used to create the derivative, otherwise a license violation has occurred.

Learning Objectives	Essential Knowledge
LO 7.3.1 Analyze the beneficial and harmful effects of computing.	**EK 7.3.1F** Open source and licensing of software and content raise legal and ethical concerns.

Practice Test 2

AP® Computer Science Principles Examination
Time: 120 minutes
Number of questions: 74

DIRECTIONS: Each of the questions below is followed by four suggested answers. For each question select the best response. For multiple-select questions, choose the two best responses.

1. A location in a computer's memory is given a hexadecimal address, which can be noted with a "0x" prefix. What is the binary value corresponding to the memory location 0x1AB4?
   (A) 0001101010110100
   (B) 0001010101011100
   (C) 0000110101011010
   (D) 0001110110101000

2. Which of the following is commonly referred to by the hex value 32CD3?
   I. The color with an RGB value (50,205,50)
   II. The width and height of a compressed image.
   III. A location in the computer's memory

   (A) I only
   (B) II only
   (C) III only
   (D) Both I and III

3. Which of the following are examples of abstraction? Select two answers.
   (A) A programmer has code to find the area of several triangles, one at a time. She decides to simplify her code by writing a procedure called "triangleArea," which takes the base and height of each triangle as a parameter.
   (B) A programmer has an error in her code, and rewrites the code so she can see every line, one at a time.
   (C) A computer science student compares two hexadecimal values.
   (D) A logic gate is used to find the difference between two integers.

4. Which of the following is not an advantage of using simulation to solve a problem?
   (A) The best solution can be found quickly.
   (B) The simulation may save money compared to constructing a physical system.
   (C) The simulation may save time compared to constructing a physical system.
   (D) The simulation may create new questions.

5. A group of students wants to ask their school to consider delaying the start time in the morning due to research they found on teenagers and the need for sleep. The school has agreed to share anonymous data with the students to help them make a recommendation. What data will be helpful to the students?
   (A) Average grades of students taking the same classes at different times in the day over several years.
   (B) Results of a student survey.
   (C) Absence statistics over several years.
   (D) Tardiness statistics over several years.

6. Which of the following is <u>not</u> true about hypotheses?
   (A) The results of a simulation may or may not generate a new hypothesis.
   (B) Hypotheses can be tested with a simulation.
   (C) It is usually less expensive to test a hypothesis by collecting real-time data than to create a model.
   (D) Hypotheses explain the model being tested.

7. How many distinct values can we represent with 5 bits of data?
   (A) 5
   (B) 16
   (C) 32
   (D) 64

8. Which base is an abstraction of the way that information flows through a computer?
   (A) binary
   (B) octal
   (C) decimal
   (D) hexadecimal

9. How many binary digits are needed to write the value of 500?
   (A) 8
   (B) 9
   (C) 10
   (D) 11

10. In some computing systems, a leading 0 in a digit entered is assumed to be octal. For example, 010, will be converted to 8_{10}. In the following set of numbers, assume that the numbers are base ten, unless they have a leading zero. Find the decimal sum of the following numbers: 3, 03, 4, and 015.
    (A) 20
    (B) 23
    (C) 44
    (D) 56

11. Calvin has been gathering data for a few weeks for a paper in his statistics class. He has put the data into a spreadsheet and is now ready to create a visual representation of his findings. Calvin's research consisted of polling his fellow students on their favorite movie genres. He now wants to present a graphic displaying the percentage of students that favor each genre. Which of the graphs/charts below would NOT be suitable for this kind of visualization?

(A)

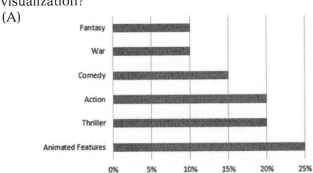

(B)

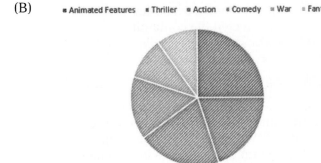

(C)

(D)

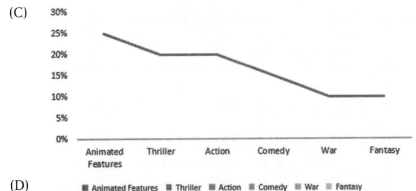

12. As part of Calvin's research, he came across a national study from five years earlier that gathered data similar to his. As a conclusion to his paper he wants to summarize the findings of the two studies. Which of the following could possibly be a good summary statement of his research? Select <u>two</u> answers.
    (A) Five years ago the most popular genre of movie amongst high school students was comedy. Now animated movies take the top spot.
    (B) Movie watching patterns among teenagers are substantially different than they were five years ago.
    (C) The types of movies watched by high school students has changed due to the increased availability of online movie streaming sites.
    (D) The types of movies that teenagers prefer to watch has changed over the last 5 years. Favorites include animation, thriller and action as opposed to comedy, mystery, and romance.

13. Which of the following would NOT be considered a large dataset that can be digitally manipulated? Select <u>two</u> answers.
    (A) A music streaming service's digital music catalogue.
    (B) A personal digital password-protected file containing addresses of family and friends.
    (C) Data downloaded from a government website.
    (D) The digital photos on a cell phone.

14. Maddie is doing research on the federal student financial aid system. She goes to a government website and finds a data set that includes information from every college, university, and technical and vocational institution that participates in the federal student financial aid programs. Datasets include year-over-year enrollments, program completions, graduation rates, faculty and staff, finances, institutional prices, and student financial aid. The data is delivered as a spreadsheet on her tablet to do the data analysis. Why is a tablet not the best choice for this task?
    (A) The storage capacity of the tablet may not support the amount of data that is in the dataset.
    (B) The tablet's spreadsheet program may not be able to process the data and analyze it properly.
    (C) The network transmission of the data set may require a connection that the tablet will not support.
    (D) The dataset may require a format conversion before the data analysis can proceed.

15. In order to properly analyze data sets, the data must be in a format that is usable for various file contents and search parameters. For the purpose of data set analysis, which of the following is LEAST related to all of the others structurally?
    (A) A compilation of digital music files with limited metadata.
    (B) A frequency analysis of brief messages, blogs, and other social media posts.
    (C) A digital image library made up of various image formats.
    (D) A collection of digital video files set up for a streaming service.

16. When working with large data sets, scalability of a system plays a vital role. What does scalability mean?
    (A) The ability of a system to increase its size exponentially without the need for additional hardware.
    (B) The capability of a system, network, or process to handle a growing amount of work, or its potential to be enlarged in order to accommodate that growth.
    (C) The capability of a system to self-regulate and limit the amount of information that flows through it to ensure that the system is not overloaded.
    (D) The ability of a system to process complex information by turning it into smaller packets called granules, enabling the system to process the information better.

17. Analytics is the computational analysis of data. There are many types of analytics that people can use to properly process large data sets. Which of the following analytics type is defined incorrectly?
    (A) Operationalized – analytics that become part of the business process.
    (B) Basic – analytics used for data manipulation, simple visualizations, and monitoring.
    (C) Monetized – analytics that require fees to be paid in order to access and process the data.
    (D) Advanced – analytics used for predictive modeling and pattern matching.

18. Which of the following is the least relevant consideration when deciding on a data storage format?
    (A) Can the data storage format handle the data volume and data streaming speeds?
    (B) Is the storage format flexible enough for a variety of user needs?
    (C) Can analysis or visualization software use the storage format?
    (D) Will the storage format be the best option after several years of working with the data?

19. The question below uses a robot in a grid of squares. The robot is represented by a triangle, which is initially positioned in the upper left corner, facing toward the right side of the grid. Consider the following program segment, which is intended to move the robot to the bottom right hand block, facing right.

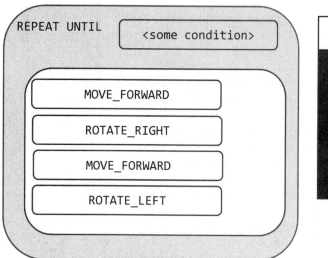

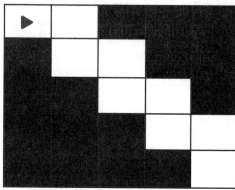

What code should replace <some condition> so that the program will work as intended?

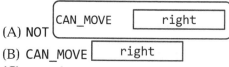

(A) NOT CAN_MOVE right

(B) CAN_MOVE right

(C) n = 4

(D) The program will terminate before the robot reaches its final position.

20. Consider the goal of finding the average of 10 random numbers between the values of 1 and 12.

I. ```
    REPEAT 10 TIMES
    {
    sum ← 0
    sum ← sum + RANDOM(1,12)
    }
    average ← sum / 10
    ```

II. ```
    sum ← 0
    REPEAT 10 TIMES
    {
    sum ← sum + RANDOM(1,12)
    }
    average ← sum / 10
    ```

(A) Algorithm I

(B) Algorithm II

(C) Algorithms I and II

(D) Neither Algorithm I nor II

21. A school has created a large community garden, and the president of the student garden club wants to create a mobile application to guide guests through the garden. She is considering what language to use. What is the most important consideration when choosing the best language to use for writing the app?
    (A) The student should choose whatever language she feels most comfortable with, because all algorithms can be expressed in any language.
    (B) The student should choose a text-based language to ensure proper sequencing, selection, and iteration.
    (C) The student should choose a block-based language to ensure quicker distribution to all members of the community.
    (D) The student should use a language specifically developed for mobile applications, because it may have some built-in functions to make the language better-suited for expressing her algorithms.

22. When choosing a programming language, which of the following will <u>not</u> be determined by the choice of language?
    (A) The clarity and readability of the code.
    (B) The data structures available.
    (C) The syntax highlighting options available.
    (D) Whether or not a solution exists.

23. Consider the following incomplete program, which is intended to move a robot forward as far as possible:

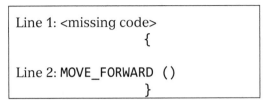

```
Line 1: <missing code>
                {

Line 2: MOVE_FORWARD  ()
                }
```

Before:

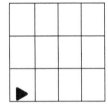

After:

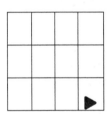

What code should replace the <missing code> ?
(A) REPEAT 4 TIMES
(B) REPEAT 3 TIMES
(C) REPEAT UNTIL (NOT CAN_MOVE (forward))
(D) REPEAT UNTIL (CAN_MOVE (forward))

24. Two students are playing a game where one student, the "guesser," is trying to guess a number from a pre-established interval that the other student, the "chooser," has written down on a piece of paper. What is true about the game?
   I.   Given enough unrepeated guesses, the guesser will ultimately select the chooser's number.
   II. The guesser will guess the chooser's number sooner if the guesser chooses consecutive numbers.
   III. The larger the pre-established interval, the longer it will likely take the guesser to select the correct answer.

   (A) I only
   (B) I and II only
   (C) I and III only
   (D) II and III only

25. A group of friends is planning a road trip from Austin, Texas to Kansas City, Missouri. At some point in their trip, either on the way there or on the way back, they want to visit the following cities:

    Dallas, Texas
    Oklahoma City, Oklahoma
    Topeka, Kansas

    They want to plan the quickest route, avoiding tolls, and finding inexpensive housing along the way. Which of the following <u>must</u> be true?
    (A) The optimal route can be found by using existing online software, plugging each location into a map.
    (B) The solution to this problem does not exist.
    (C) While an efficient solution may be possible, the group may never know if the route they selected was the best.
    (D) Taking one city out off the list makes the problem solvable in a reasonable amount of time.

26. A mother has dropped her children off at school, and must get to work on time. She relies on a map application on her mobile phone to detect traffic delays and plan her route. Which of the following are true? Select <u>two</u> answers.
    (A) The map application may or may not give her the fastest possible route to work, but will most likely eliminate the slowest routes, and will most likely provide a reasonable route.
    (B) The map application will give her the fastest route at the given moment, but delays that are reported to the application after she initially finds her route will interfere with its accuracy.
    (C) The map application, using crowd-sourcing from its users, can continuously re-route her from her current route to the best possible route if there are unexpected changes to traffic patterns.
    (D) The map application will find an approximate solution, as finding the exact solution would take too much time.

27. A team of students is programming a robot to find its way out of a maze (exact layout unknown) for a national competition. The robot will be timed, and teams with the best times will move on to the next level of the competition. What strategy should the team take?
    (A) Have the robot create a virtual map of the maze, return to the starting position, calculate the quickest route, and take it.
    (B) Program the robot to move at maximum speed, turning left or right at random until it finds the end.
    (C) Use a language most appropriate to the problem at hand, and use built-in functions, such as rotate(RIGHT) and move(), to have the robot complete the task.
    (D) Create an algorithm which, although not finding the ideal solution, finds a reasonable solution quickly.

28. Which of the following best describes an undecidable problem?
    (A) Heuristic methods are used to find a reasonable, but not the best, solution.
    (B) No algorithm can be constructed that always leads to a correct yes-or-no answer.
    (C) A binary sequence may or may not be applied correctly, given the particular data set.
    (D) Some data sets are so large that it is impossible for computing tools to facilitate the discovery of connections in information.

29. A museum is planning a large exhibit of rare gems from around the world. As one of several security precautions, the museum asks a programmer to write software that would guarantee to notify the museum of any outsider attempting to access sensitive information about the gems. The programmer could not make this guarantee. Why not?
    (A) The programmer is an outsider himself, and cannot promise that his team will not have access to the data.
    (B) Although the programmer can safeguard against many common cyber-attacks, he cannot know all ways a malicious programmer will attempt to access the information.
    (C) The programmer cannot guarantee that he could complete such a large task before the exhibit; he would prefer to take the time to create a solid piece of software that the museum can use for all exhibits.
    (D) The programmer cannot be confident that the algorithm for his program works until someone from the outside actually attempts to access the information.

30. A mathematician is working with a programmer to write a program to solve a problem using high level mathematics. The mathematician asks the programmer to help her determine the efficiency of the algorithm. How can the efficiency be determined? Select two answers.
    (A) Multiple inputs can be tested to determine how much cpu time would be required for the algorithm to solve the problem for inputs of different sizes.
    (B) Ensure that all inputs are limited in complexity.
    (C) Count the number of statements in the program.
    (D) Multiple inputs of various sizes and with different expected outputs can be tested to determine the behavior of the algorithm.

31. A small business hires a programmer to write a program for its unique needs. The programmer knows that many of the business clients are using older home computers, so the efficiency of the program's algorithm is of the utmost importance. Which of the following procedures demonstrates empirical analysis of two algorithms?

   I.   The program is run on various machines, and a clock is used to time the programs written with the algorithms.
   II. Several users test the two programs, and log how long it takes their CPUs to complete the tasks.
   III. Use pre-existing formulas to determine run-time complexity.

   (A) I only
   (B) II only
   (C) I and II
   (D) I, II, and III

32. A mother is teaching her young children about different types of fruit, specifically bananas and oranges. She uses a blocks-based language to create a game. She uses an invention kit to connect and map a real orange to the letter 'o' and a real banana to the letter 'b'. Her code is below:

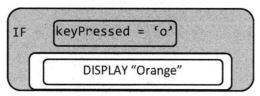

   What would be an appropriate way to finish the code segment?
   (A)

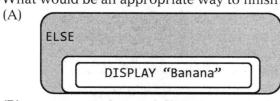

   (B)

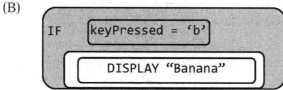

   (C)

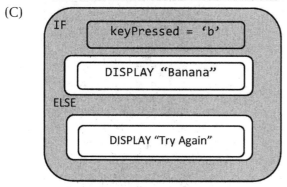

   (D) The code is complete as is.

33. Inspired by a tip-calculating mobile application that she made in the classroom, a student is inspired to create a program that uses percentages. She notices on a social media website that there is much debate over a local sales tax increase. She decides to create a calculator that will take in how much a user spends, what the current tax is, and what the future amount will be. The app will tell the user how much more the goods will cost with the new tax than the old tax. One of the procedures in her program, which finds the difference between the old and new tax, is listed below.

```
PROCEDURE taxman (category, cost)
{
  IF(category = "clothes")
{
  old ← cost * .05
  new ← cost * .06
}
IF(category = "food")
{
  old ← 0
  new ← cost * .06
}
IF(category = "other")
{
  old ← cost * .05
  new ← cost * .0725
}
RETURN (new - old)
}
```

What is returned by a call to taxman ("food", 1.00)
(A) .01
(B) .0225
(C) .06
(D) .60

34. Consider the following procedure:

```
PROCEDURE chatGreeting (feeling)
{
  IF (words = "happy")
  {
     DISPLAY ("Greetings!")
     DISPLAY ("Today is going to be a great day!")
     DISPLAY ("Glad you are well!")
     DISPLAY ("Thanks for chatting!")
  }
  ELSE
  {
     DISPLAY ("Greetings!")
     DISPLAY ("Today is going to be a great day!")
     DISPLAY ("Hope things look better for you
later!")
     DISPLAY ("Thanks for chatting!")
  }
}
```

How could this code <u>best</u> be made more efficient?
(A) Place the if and else conditions at the beginning, followed by all DISPLAY statements.
(B) Place the if and else conditions at the end, after all DISPLAY statements.
(C) Place the if and else conditions in the middle of the code, after the "Today is going to be a great day!" DISPLAY statement but before the one differing statement.
(D) The code is efficient as is.

35. A team of students is collaborating on a program to obtain local weather data from a website, and predict weather-related school closings based on their own formulas. They must present their code to a group of faculty, some of whom have little to no experience with code. What strategies can the group use while writing their code, in order to make it more understandable for the faculty? Select <u>two</u> answers.
(A) Choose meaningful names for all variables and procedures.
(B) Include comments detailing previous, unsuccessful coding attempts.
(C) Use shorter blocks of code wherever possible.
(D) Repeat blocks of code to emphasize their importance in the process.

36. An entrepreneur has hired a programmer to design software to take user input and convert it to appear a certain way. The programmer is not clear on the assignment, so he asks the entrepreneur to elaborate. What can the programmer ask the entrepreneur to do to make the assignment more clear?
    (A) Give some examples of user input and what the result should look like.
    (B) Write some sample code to show the programmer exactly what he wants.
    (C) Sit side-by side throughout the debugging process.
    (D) Select the most appropriate language for the application.

37. An artist is using a programming language to make an interactive piece of art. He elects to keep his code private, to protect his work from imitation. Although they do not affect how his code runs, which of the following will make his code easier to edit in the future? Select two answers.
    (A) Adequate and appropriate comments
    (B) Syntax of the language
    (C) Testing of the code with various inputs
    (D) Naming conventions

38. What measures can a programmer take to help ensure that a program produces correct output? Select two answers.
    (A) Test multiple inputs on the program.
    (B) Find the efficiency of the code.
    (C) Develop the program in smaller steps, ensuring each step is correct.
    (D) Calculate the time it takes to run the program.

39. A group of high school students is participating in a mobile application development contest. They have a limited time frame, and would like to add many features. Which of the following strategies will allow them to create the best app they can in the time allotted?

    Strategy I: The students outline all goals. They make a program with all procedure names. They use software to simultaneously work on different parts of the code, frequently compiling and testing all code together. As each individual student completes one procedure, that student moves onto the next procedure.

    Strategy II: The students outline all goals. They work together on some shared code, and students work with their own copies of the code on specific parts. They check in regularly, and completed, correct code is added to a master program.

    (A) Strategy I only
    (B) Strategy II only
    (C) Strategy I and Strategy II will allow the students to create a quality application.
    (D) Neither Strategy I nor Strategy II will allow the students to create a quality application.

40. A mobile application developer would like to create an app that searches and sorts a list, vacationCosts, in several ways. One step of his project involves copying values from vacationCosts into an empty list called expensiveVacations, which includes only values greater than 750. Which of the following code segments will create a new list, with only the larger values?

    I. ```
    FOR EACH item IN vacationCosts
    {
      IF (item > 750)
      {
        APPEND (expensiveVacations, item)
      }
    }
    ```

    II. ```
    FOR EACH item IN vacationCosts
    {
      IF (vacationCosts[item] > 750)
      {
        APPEND (expensiveVacations,
    vacationCosts[item])
      }
    }
    ```

    (A) I only
    (B) II only
    (C) I and II
    (D) Neither I nor II

41. Which of the following is <u>NOT</u> true about program documentation?
    (A) The Digital Millennium Copyright Act requires that all documentation for published programs is available, while protecting artists and programmers.
    (B) Program documentation helps programmers develop and maintain correct programs to efficiently solve problems.
    (C) Program documentation about program components helps in developing and maintaining programs.
    (D) Program documentation helps while working collaboratively in programming environments.

42. The following question uses a robot in a grid of squares. Which of the following will cause the robot code to stop executing?
    (A) The robot is stuck with nowhere to move.
    (B) The robot is in an infinite loop.
    (C) The condition in an "if" statement is not met.
    (D) The robot attempts to move off its grid.

43. The following question uses a robot in a grid of squares. Consider the code segment below:

```
REPEAT UNTIL (NOT CAN_MOVE(right))
{
  IF(CAN_MOVE (forward))
  {
    MOVE_FORWARD()
  }
  IF(NOT CAN_MOVE (forward))
  {
    ROTATE_RIGHT ()
    ROTATE_RIGHT ()
    MOVE_FORWARD()
  }
}
```

For the following initial situation, what will be the final position and direction of the robot after the code is executed?

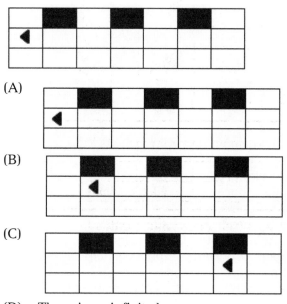

(A)

(B)

(C)

(D)   There is an infinite loop.

44. The following question uses a robot in a grid of squares. Consider writing code to bring the robot from the top left hand corner of a grid to the bottom right. For example:

Before:	After:

What type of control structure is MOST appropriate for this program?
(A) IF (condition)
(B) REPEAT n TIMES
(C) REPEAT UNTIL (condition)
(D) FOR EACH item IN list

45. The following question uses a robot in a grid of squares. Consider the following procedure:

```
PROCEDURE navigate (directionList)
{
 steps ← 0
  FOR EACH direction IN directionList
  {
    IF (direction = right)
    {
      ROTATE_RIGHT ()
    }
    IF (direction = left)
    {
ROTATE_RIGHT ()
ROTATE_RIGHT ()
ROTATE_RIGHT ()
          }
    IF (direction = forward)
    {
      steps ← steps + 1
    }
    IF (direction = backward)
    {
      steps ← steps - 1
    }
  }
IF (steps < 0)
{
    stepsBack ← steps * -1
    ROTATE_RIGHT ()
    ROTATE_RIGHT ()
    REPEAT stepsBack TIMES
    {
      MOVE_FORWARD ()
    }
}
}
```

For the following initial situation, what will be the final position and direction of the robot after the code is executed?

```
directionList = {forward, forward, right, left,
left, right, right, backward, backward, backward}
```

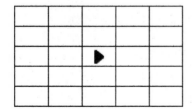

(A)

(B)

(C)

(D)

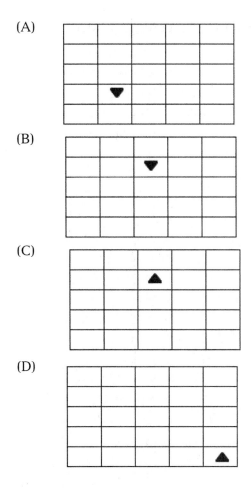

46. An introductory computer science student is creating a "late server" program which calculates how much money to leave at a table if the server has not been to the table for a long period of time, and the customer must leave. Consider the following instructions. Assume that mealTotal, taxRate (as a percent) and tipRate (as a percent) have all been input correctly. How can the instructions I-IV be sequenced correctly? Select <u>two</u> answers.
I.   mealTotal ← mealTotal + tip + tax
II.   tip ← mealTotal * tipRate / 100
III. tax ← meal Total * taxRate / 100
IV. DISPLAY mealTotal

(A) I, II, III, IV
(B) I, III, II, IV
(C) II, III, I, IV
(D) III, II, I, IV

47. Which of the following is NOT a use of application programming interfaces (APIs)?
(A) Allowing software components to communicate.
(B) Simplifying complex programming tasks.
(C) Justifying a program's correctness.
(D) Sharing a library of available procedures.

48. Which of the following code segments will display: 1 2 4 8 16 ?

   I.
```
num ← 1
REPEAT 5 TIMES
  {
        num ← num * 2
      DISPLAY (num)
  }
```

   II.
```
num ← 1
REPEAT UNTIL (num ≥ 16)
  {
    DISPLAY (num)
    num ← num * 2
  }
```

   III.
```
num ← 1
REPEAT UNTIL (num > 16)
  {
    DISPLAY (num)
    num ← num * 2
  }
```

(A) II only
(B) I and II
(C) II and III
(D) I, II, and III

49. A student is creating a budget, and evaluating his purchases over the last month. Consider the following code segment which attempts to find the sum of all purchases made in the last month, stored in purchaseList.

```
n ← 1
sum ← 0
REPEAT UNTIL (<missing code>)
{
  sum ← sum + purchaseList[n]
  n ← n + 1
}
```

What code can replace missing code to assign the total of all values in purchaseList to sum?

I.   `n = LENGTH[purchaseList]`
II. `n ≥ LENGTH[purchaseList]`
III. `n > LENGTH[purchaseList]`

(A) II only
(B) III only
(C) I, II and III
(D) II and III

50. A researcher has accidentally copied a list. Before he deletes the copy, he wants to make sure that the two lists are identical, and that he has not made edits to the incorrect list. He verifies that list1 and list2 are the same length. Consider the following procedure, which attempts to return a Boolean value of true if the lists are identical and false otherwise.

```
PROCEDURE listCheck (list1, list2)
{
  <missing code>
  {
    IF (list1[n] = list2[n])
    {
      RETURN false
    }
  }
  RETURN true
}
```

What could replace <missing code> to ensure that the code returns the proper result?

I.   `n = LENGTH [list1]`
     `REPEAT n TIMES`
II. `FOR EACH n IN list1`

(A) I only
(B) II only
(C) I and II
(D) Neither I nor II

51. Review the URL below.

    https://widgets.com/products/catalog.asp

Which of the following accurately identifies the highlighted sections of the web address, in the proper order?
(A) domain, top level domain, file extension
(B) protocol, domain, webpage
(C) security, domain, file folder
(D) protocol, top level domain, directory

52. The number of people using the Internet worldwide has exploded. The proliferation of devices that are Internet-capable has required the development of new protocols so there are enough IP addresses for those devices. The old IPv4 system was a 32-bit based system, while the new IPv6 system is a 128-bit system. Based on the difference in the two systems, select the answer below that accurately reflects the numbers of available IP addresses for each system.
(A) IPv4: 32^{10}, IPv6: 128^{10}
(B) IPv4: 2^{32}, IPv6: 2^{128}
(C) IPv4: 32^{2}, IPv6: 128^{2}
(D) IPv4: 10^{32}, IPv6: 10^{128}

53. Internet Protocol (IPv4) addresses are broken down into parts. What are the two primary parts of an IPv4 address?
    (A) network host and subnet ID
    (B) network prefix and host identifier
    (C) physical address and logical address
    (D) subnet mask and node prefix

54. Suppose that two people, Allison and Nate, want to send each other messages via the internet. Allison sends a message to Nate using no encryption other than Nate's public key. What is the most likely scenario?
    (A) A person trying to hack Nate's messages will find accessing his messages easy to accomplish.
    (B) Nate can be assured that Allison was the sender of the message.
    (C) Nate will be the only person able to read the message.
    (D) Nate can reply to Allison and only she will be able to read the reply.

55. One day while going through your e-mail, you see an e-mail that appears to be from your favorite local store offering a 75% discount for all online purchases made from a special link located at the bottom of the e-mail message. Which of the following links is LEAST likely to make you a victim of a social engineering scam?
    (A) https://site.widgetworld.com/offer
    (B) http://widgetworld.com.site/offer
    (C) https://widgetworld.com/siteoffer
    (D) http://site.widgetworld.com/offer

56. You are doing an internship with network security firm, working with a team investigating a breach of a local bank's data center. During the meetings to discuss the possible methods that the hackers used to breach the system, many people have ideas. Which of the following are viable possibilities for the data breach? Select two answers.
    (A) The hackers used an exploit in the bank's online banking system to gain access to the data.
    (B) The hackers used a rootkit to gain access to the bank's data center.
    (C) The hackers utilized a form of social engineering to trick a bank employee into giving them login information to the bank's mainframe.
    (D) The hackers utilized a wildcard which is a form of universal password that may or may not be able to access major computing systems around the world.

57. When looking at a URL, it might be easier to think of the addressing structure as a type of tree. The elements of a URL (or the collection of elements) form branches that lead from one place to another and can sometimes merge back together. Consider the following URL:

https://www.widgets.com/products/woozies/list.asp?x=1&y=2

Which part of the URL is *least* like a branch of a tree?
(A) https://
(B) www.widgets.com
(C) products/woozies
(D) list.asp?

58. You are asked to speak to a group of 5th and 6th graders about being safe while they are on the Internet. You decide to focus your presentation on how to ensure online safety when the kids are using age-appropriate Massive Multiplayer Online Role Playing Games (MMORPGs). Which of the guidelines below are appropriate? Select <u>two</u> answers.
(A) Do not use the game's chat feature to talk to people you don't know and do not give anyone any of your real life information.
(B) Do not tell your friends your username and when you will be online.
(C) When playing any online games, be wary of anyone who is constantly asking you to friend them in the game. If you do not know them in real life, don't friend them in the game.
(D) When playing online games, do not accept any quests that require you to play with other people. All quests that require multiple players are not appropriate.

59. Many companies have network protections in place to prevent outside access to their network. This is often done by means of a firewall. Which of the following statements below is *not* true of firewalls?
(A) A firewall is a piece of hardware or software designed to filter packets going into and out of your network.
(B) A firewall can go into your network after it has been compromised, identify threats that do not meet its established rules and remove the threat from your system.
(C) A firewall retrieves the information from the Internet, processes it to ensure it meets the standards set, and then sends the information to the requesting system.
(D) A firewall can scan the contents of packets as they come through the system with respect to a set of rules created by the private network owner. Packets adhering to the rules are allowed in, while other are discarded.

60. The DNS system is designed to be very scalable and allows for top level domains to be broken down into subdomains and those subsequently broken down into further subdomains. Examples of top level domains are .com, .org, and .us. You have taken ownership of the widgets.org subdomain and you wish to create additional subdomains within widgets.org. Which of the following contain valid subdomains for widgets.org? Select <u>two</u> answers.
    (A) widgets.org/east; widgets.org/west; widgets.org/northwest
    (B) east.widgets.org; west.widgets.org; northwest.widgets.org
    (C) round.widgets.org; newyork.east.widgets.org
    (D) widgets.org.southwest; widgets.org.east; widgets.org.west.fresno

61. Your family gives an elderly family member a new laptop for her birthday. You decide that rather than overwhelm her with all of the things that she can do, you want her to learn only one basic thing that will allow her to keep in touch with her family and friends. Which of the following would be the easiest option for your family member to start with?
    (A) Have her set up a profile on a social networking website so she can converse with friends and family through that site.
    (B) Help her set up an email account with the appropriate security settings so she can email friends and family and get used to how her computer works.
    (C) Help her set up a digital blog so she can starting writing a daily journal of her activities for friends and family to read.
    (D) Help her setup an IRC account so she can text and chat with family in real time.

62. Bill has just received his degree in education and he is looking for locations that might have the most teaching positions available. He has talked to his college advisor but he did not receive enough information. What would be the most efficient way for Bill to find which parts of his state have a need for new teachers?
    (A) Conduct a web search for all teacher openings in his state
    (B) Utilize an available data set from the U.S. government regarding teacher shortages in various states
    (C) Consult with a job search firm and pay them a fee to locate possible positions
    (D) Go to his public library and look through employment classified ads in local newspapers

63. While walking around his classroom, a teacher sees a student on a website that is on the school's blacklist. He advises the student to close the site and not to access it in the future. What are the most likely ways that the student bypassed the school's web filter? Select two answers.
    (A) The student was able to hack into the school's filtering software and turn it off.
    (B) The student used a proxy server which tricks the school's server and web filter into allowing blocked content.
    (C) The student brought his own laptop and connected it to the school's student Wi-Fi. Because it was the student's personal laptop, the filtering did not take effect.
    (D) The student activated a portable hot spot on his cell phone and connected the computer to the web using his cellular data plan.

64. An archaeologist is studying Native American ruins in the American Southwest. He has recently found a previously unknown settlement and wishes to share the find with his research partner who is off-site. Which of the following would be the best method of both documenting his discovery and allowing his research partner to participate and view the settlement in real time?
    (A) Use a digital camera to take pictures of the site and upload the pictures to a cloud server with notes attached to each file.
    (B) Using a digital sketch pad, sketch the artifacts that are found and send the sketches along with notes and some photos to the research partner via email.
    (C) Use a real-time conferencing application on a tablet to allow his research partner to "see" the site and the artifacts along with him. Record the conversation for later review and joint note-taking.
    (D) Call his research partner on a cell phone and do a verbal walkthrough of the site. Describe the artifacts and send digital pictures later after the call.

65. Mrs. Morgan is an elementary school teacher in a small, rural town. Her school's technology budget is very limited but she wants to use technology to enhance her instruction. Below is a list of actions she takes to utilize technology in her classroom. Which of these actions were legal under copyright law?
    I. She makes a compilation CD (anthology) from her personal CD collection
    II. She records a documentary from TV and shows the video to her class the next day before having a class discussion.
    III. She makes photocopies of a page from a geography coloring book to include in a class worksheet.
    IV. She buys a copy of an educational software title and loads it on all of the computers in her classroom.
    V. She allows her students to print out pages from a CD-based encyclopedia for research purposes.

    (A) II, V
    (B) I, III, IV
    (C) II, III, V
    (D) None of the above are legal.

66. Which of the following statements support the idea that the Internet and World Wide Web have made positive impacts on the global society?
    I. Online educational opportunities have increased substantially year after year, which is giving more people the chance to pursue higher education.
    II. The ability of private persons to sell items online has created a new form of commerce that has never been seen before.
    III. Peer to peer networks have allowed individuals across the world to trade commercially made digital products more easily than ever before.
    IV. Video streaming sites have allowed both commercial and independent movie producers to get their films seen by more viewers at lower distribution costs.

    (A) II, IV
    (B) I, II, IV
    (C) I, III, IV
    (D) All of the above

67. A family has decided to take a trip to Ireland to explore their family history. The mother decides to use a popular online travel site to check airfare and hotel rates. Because she is just starting her search, she does not create an account for the site. A few days later she revisits the site to purchase the airline tickets and make hotel reservations. After the Web page loads, she notices several advertisements for various Irish tourist attractions. Which of the following MOST likely explains how the site was able to target the advertising to her?
    (A) The site accessed information about her last visit from a cookie placed on her machine previously.
    (B) Her browser history was accessed by the site on this most recent visit and was able to determine her previous search history.
    (C) The site was able to access information about her last visit from the web server.
    (D) The advertiser was able to track her and identified her as a potential customer.

68. Over a summer break three college students who were all computer science majors happen to meet and strike up a conversation about various mobile applications they wanted to develop. After several conversations and a few development meetings the students all went back to their respective schools which were spread across the country. Which of the following is the BEST method the three could use to continue to develop their mobile applications?
    (A) The students could all create accounts on a cloud-based project management site which allows for project development, file sharing, version control, and real-time collaboration.
    (B) The students can set up dates and times for video conference calls to each other and discuss their individual progress on the mobile apps.
    (C) The students could e-mail updated versions of their mobile applications back and forth until they have completed their projects.
    (D) Each student could make screen capture videos of themselves working on their piece of the project, then post them to a video upload service so the others can watch the video and hear the commentary.

69. Computer artifacts comes in many forms. This includes pictures, programs, music files, etc. Programmers can use these artifacts to conceal various other files, by hiding data within data (a practice known as steganography). Review the options below and select the option that is NOT an example of steganography.
    (A) Sending a virus disguised as a valid e-mail attachment such as an image, document, or spreadsheet.
    (B) Embedding pictures into a video file; the video is played at a slower speed and the image(s) are revealed.
    (C) Hiding audio messages within another audio signal that is self-executing.
    (D) Using hidden characters and redundant markup language to embed information in the HTML of a webpage.

70. A geocacher hobbyist uses sets of coordinates to locate hidden caches all over the country. In order to be an effective geocacher, a person must have an understanding of global positioning systems. Which of the following is NOT true of GPS systems?
    (A) Basemaps need to be updated periodically.
    (B) Some topographic features such as mountains and canyons can hinder GPS signals.
    (C) GPS systems are accurate to within a few hundred feet.
    (D) Russia, China, and Europe have their own versions of GPS systems.

71. As movies and music have moved into the digital world, the legal protections that relate to them have had to continually evolve. Which of the following best describes how the legal landscape regarding digital movies and music has changed?
    (A) The music and movie industries have chosen to protect their copyrights by filing lawsuits against people who share digital files without permission
    (B) Copyright laws related to digital content have been modified and simplified so that they are easier to understand.
    (C) The music and movie industries have actively promoted peer to peer sharing sites as a way to control how digital content is used.
    (D) United States lawmakers have chosen to take a wait-and-see position on the legal issues related to digital media.

72. Which of the following statements best describes the relationship between open source software and free software?
    (A) Free software is provided free of cost but the source code is not available to the user; open source makes the source code available to the user for modification and redistribution.
    (B) Open source is source code that is publicly available under a license and users can change and distribute the software as they wish; free software is source code you can modify and redistribute with no legal restraints.
    (C) Free software is code that is made available for consumer use only and commercial use of any kind is prohibited; open source is source code made available for commercial use only.
    (D) There is no difference—the two concepts and terms are interchangeable.

73. Which of the following are examples of digital collaboration tools that a junior high teacher could use to enhance the digital collaboration of her students?
    I.   A free tool that allows users to easily create bubble maps that can be exported in various formats, saved, and edited collaboratively.
    II. Creating flowcharts and diagrams online using a real-time collaboration website.
    III. A free productivity application that helps students organize personal schedules and to-do lists.
    IV. An app allowing users to review, annotate, share and discuss the content on any Web page.
    V.   An app that lets people work on one document simultaneously, and allows users to create a "team space" on their own private subdomain for free.

    (A) I & II
    (B) IV & V
    (C) I, II, IV, & V
    (D) All of the above

74. There are several technology systems in place at Johnson High School. Which of the following systems will provide a cost savings for the school district by virtue of being fully automated? Select two answers.
    (A) A motion detection and timer system in the classroom that turns the classroom lights off and on based on movement detected in the classroom.
    (B) A card swipe system in the cafeteria that allows the cafeteria workers to make deposits and withdraws from a student's meal account.
    (C) An RFID system built into the student ID badges that allows a computerized system to track student movement and locate students in case of emergency.
    (D) A high definition camera system throughout the school that allows one centrally located security officer to have a "view" of the entire school and send security personnel to specific locations within the school if the need arises.

ANSWERS FOR MULTIPLE-CHOICE QUESTIONS

1. **Answer: A.** We must convert from hexadecimal to binary: 1 converts to 0001, A to 1010, B to 1011, and 4 to 0100.

Learning Objectives	Essential Knowledge
LO 2.1.1 Describe the variety of abstractions used to represent data.	**EK 2.1.1A** Digital data is represented by abstractions at different levels.
	EK 2.1.1C At a higher level, bits are grouped to represent abstractions, including but not limited to numbers, characters, and color.
	EK 2.1.1D Number bases, including binary, decimal, and hexadecimal, are used to represent and investigate digital data.
	EK 2.1.1E At one of the lowest levels of abstraction, digital data is represented in binary (base 2) using only combinations of the digits zero and one.
	EK 2.1.1F Hexadecimal (base 16) is used to represent digital data because hexadecimal representation uses fewer digits than binary.
	EK 2.1.1G Numbers can be converted from any base to any other base.

2. **Answer: D.** Two of the things that hexadecimal can be used for are color and memory addresses.

Learning Objectives	Essential Knowledge
LO 2.1.1 Describe the variety of abstractions used to represent data.	**EK 2.1.1C** At a higher level, bits are grouped to represent abstractions, including but not limited to numbers, characters, and color.
LO 2.1.2 Explain how binary sequences are used to represent digital data.	**EK 2.1.2D** The interpretation of a binary sequence depends on how it is used.
	EK 2.1.2E A sequence of bits may represent instructions or data.
	EK 2.1.2F A sequence of bits may represent different types of data in different contexts.

3. **Answers: A, D**. Writing a code procedure and using a logic gate both involve taking a complicated concept and simplifying it.

Learning Objectives	Essential Knowledge
LO 2.2.1 Develop an abstraction when writing a program or creating other computational artifacts.	**EK 2.2.1A** The process of developing an abstraction involves removing detail and generalizing functionality.
	EK 2.2.1B An abstraction extracts common features from specific examples in order to generalize concepts.
	EK 2.2.1C An abstraction generalizes functionality with input parameters that allow software reuse.
LO 2.2.3 Identify multiple levels of abstractions that are used when writing programs.	**EK 2.2.3F** A logic gate is a hardware abstraction that is modeled by a Boolean function.

4. **Answer: A**. While simulation may help to find a solution quickly, it is unknown if the solution is the best.

Learning Objectives	Essential Knowledge
LO 2.3.1 Use models and simulations to represent phenomena.	**EK 2.3.1C** Models often omit unnecessary features of the objects or phenomena that are being modeled.
	EK 2.3.1D Simulations mimic real-world events without the cost or danger of building and testing the phenomena in the real world.

5. **Answer: A**. For any given course, multiple data points of student performance in that class at different times of the day, and over many years, will give a more complete picture of student learning in the school.

Learning Objectives	Essential Knowledge
LO 2.3.2 Use models and simulations to formulate, refine, and test hypotheses.	**EK 2.3.2A** Models and simulations facilitate the formulation and refinement of hypotheses related to the objects of phenomena under consideration.

6. **Answer: C.** An advantage of testing hypotheses with models and simulations is that this approach usually saves time and money.

Learning Objectives	Essential Knowledge
LO 2.3.2 Use models and simulations to formulate, refine, and test hypotheses.	EK 2.3.2B Hypotheses are formulated to explain the objects or phenomena being modeled. EK 2.3.2C Hypotheses are refined by examining that insights that models and simulations provide into the objects or phenomena. EK 2.3.2D The results of simulations may generate new knowledge and new hypotheses related to the phenomena being modeled. EK 2.3.2E Simulations allow hypotheses to be tested without the constraints of the real world.

7. **Answer: C.** A bit can have only one of two values, so five bits of data can take on $2^5 = 32$ distinct values.

Learning Objectives	Essential Knowledge
LO 2.1.1 Describe the variety of abstractions used to represent data.	EK 2.1.1E At one of the lowest levels of abstraction, digital data is represented in binary (base 2) using only combinations of the digits zero and one.

8. **Answer: A.** Binary values (1s and 0s) can represent true/false, yes/no, +/-, or on/off.

Learning Objectives	Essential Knowledge
LO 2.1.1 Describe the variety of abstractions used to represent data.	EK 2.1.1A Digital data is represented by abstractions at different levels. EK 2.1.1E At one of the lowest levels of abstraction, digital data is represented in binary (base 2) using only combinations of the digits zero and one.

9. **Answer: B.** Since 500 is greater than 2^9, but less than 2^{10}, 9 digits are required. The binary equivalent of 500 is 111110100.

Learning Objectives	Essential Knowledge
LO 2.1.1 Describe the variety of abstractions used to represent data.	EK 2.1.1D Number bases, including binary, decimal, and hexadecimal, are used to represent and investigate digital data. EK 2.1.1E At one of the lowest levels of abstraction, digital data is represented in binary (base 2) using only combinations of the digits zero and one. EK 2.1.1G Numbers can be converted from any base to any other base.

10. **Answer: B**. We must rewrite the set of numbers in base ten, then find the sum. $3 + 03 + 4 + 015 = 3_{10} + 3_8 + 4_{10} + 15_8 = 3+3+4+13 = 23$.

Learning Objectives	Essential Knowledge
LO 2.1.1 Describe the variety of abstractions used to represent data.	EK 2.1.1A Digital data is represented by abstractions at different levels. EK 2.1.1G Numbers can be converted from any base to any other base.

11. **Answer: C**. The line graph is more appropriate in analyzing trends or seeing changes over time for one or more sets of data. For example, showing the change over time in popularity of animated movies would work well as a broken line graph (data points per year connected by straight line segments). Other genres could be added to that graph and represented with their own broken line plots.

Learning Objectives	Essential Knowledge
LO 3.1.3 Explain the insight and knowledge gained from digitally processed data by using appropriate visualizations, notations, and precise language.	EK 3.1.3B Tables, diagrams, and textual displays can be used in communicating insight and knowledge gained from data.

12. **Answers: A, D**. These two statements make clear, concise inferences from the results of the research and give examples of the data. Answer B is too vague, while choice C is not a conclusion one can reach merely based on a question about movie genre preferences.

Learning Objectives	Essential Knowledge
LO 3.1.3 Explain the insight and knowledge gained from digitally processed data by using appropriate visualizations, notations, and precise language.	EK 3.1.3C Summaries of data analyzed computationally can be effective in communicating insight and knowledge gained from digitally represented information.

13. **Answers: B, D**. An address list of family and friends, and a file of cell phone photos are not large datasets.

Learning Objectives	Essential Knowledge
LO 3.2.2 Determine how large data sets impact the use of computational processes to discover information and knowledge.	EK 3.2.2A Large data sets include data such as transactions, measurements, texts, sounds, images, and videos.

14. **Answer: A.** Due to the amount of data that is in the data set, the tablet may not have enough internal memory to save it. The spreadsheet program on the tablet may not be optimal but it will work. The same is true of the Wi-Fi connection used to download the data.

Learning Objectives	Essential Knowledge
LO 3.2.2 Determine how large data sets impact the use of computational processes to discover information and knowledge.	EK 3.2.2B The storing, processing, and curating of large data sets is challenging. EK 3.2.2C Structuring large data sets for analysis can be challenging. EK 3.2.2E Scalability of systems is an important consideration when data sets are large. EK 3.2.2F The size or scale of a system that stores data affects how that data set is used. EK 3.2.2H Analytical techniques to store, manage, transmit, and process data sets change as the size of data sets scale.

15. **Answer: B.** Social media files such as these are made up of poorly structured pieces of data, while the other three are structured for storage and display/playback.

Learning Objectives	Essential Knowledge
LO 3.2.2 Determine how large data sets impact the use of computational processes to discover information and knowledge.	EK 3.2.2C Structuring large data sets for analysis can be challenging.

16. **Answer: B.** Scalability is the ability of a system to be enlarged, through either software or hardware to accommodate the need to process larger amounts of data.

Learning Objectives	Essential Knowledge
LO 3.2.2 Determine how large data sets impact the use of computational processes to discover information and knowledge.	EK 3.2.2E Scalability of systems in an important consideration when data sets are large.

17. **Answer: C.** Monetized analytics are used to drive revenue, not take from it.

Learning Objectives	Essential Knowledge
LO 3.2.2 Determine how large data sets impact the use of computational processes to discover information and knowledge.	EK 3.2.2G The effective use of large data sets requires computational solutions.

18. **Answer: D**. We can reasonably assume that new data storage types will come along, and, if several years later, we need to change how our data is stored, we should be able to do so.

Learning Objectives	Essential Knowledge
LO 3.3.1 Analyze how data representation, storage, security, and transmission of data involve computational manipulation of information.	**EK 3.3.1G** Data is stored in many formats depending on its characteristics (e.g., size and intended use).

19. **Answer: A**. The robot should stop moving when, at the end of the block of statements, it cannot move forward. In this case, that will be at the bottom right of the grid.

Learning Objectives	Essential Knowledge
LO 3.1.3 Explain the insight and knowledge gained from digitally processed data by using approximations, visualizations, notations, and precise language.	**EK 3.1.3A** Visualization tools and software can communicate information about data.
LO 4.1.1 Develop an algorithm for implementation in a program.	**EK 4.1.1B** Sequencing is the application of each step of an algorithm in the order in which the statements are given. **EK 4.1.1D** Iteration is the repetition of part of an algorithm until a condition is met or for a specified number of times.
LO 4.1.2 Express an algorithm in a language.	**EK 4.1.2A** Languages for algorithms include natural language, pseudocode, and visual and textual programming languages. **EK 4.1.2B** Natural language and pseudocode describe algorithms so that humans can understand them.
LO 5.5.1 Employ appropriate mathematical and logical concepts in programming.	**EK 5.5.1G** Intuitive and formal reasoning about program components using Boolean concepts helps in developing correct programs.

20. **Answer: B**. Algorithm II adds 10 values to the sum, then divides by 10. Algorithm I keeps initializing the sum at 0 for each iteration, rather than finding a total.

Learning Objectives	Essential Knowledge
LO 4.1.2 Express an algorithm in a language.	**EK 4.1.2C** Algorithms described in programming languages can be executed on a computer.
LO 5.5.1 Employ appropriate mathematical and logical concepts in programming.	**EK 5.5.1D** Mathematical expressions using arithmetic operators are part of most programming languages.

21. **Answer: D**. A software specific to mobile application development will save the student time and energy, so she can use the built-in functions to better express her algorithms.

Learning Objectives	Essential Knowledge
LO 4.1.2 Express an algorithm in a language.	EK 4.1.2D Different languages are better suited for expressing different algorithms. EK 4.1.2E Some programming languages are designed for specific domains and are better for expressing algorithms in those domains.

22. **Answer: D**. The language itself cannot determine if a solution exists. Finding the solution is the work of the algorithm that is constructed in that language.

Learning Objectives	Essential Knowledge
LO 4.1.2 Express an algorithm in a language.	EK 4.1.2F The language used to express an algorithm can affect characteristics such as clarity or readability but not whether an algorithmic solution exists.
LO 4.2.2 Explain the difference between solvable and unsolvable problems in computer science.	EK 4.2.2D Some problems cannot be solved using any algorithm.

23. **Answer: C**. The missing code must move the robot forward as long as there is an open space ahead.

Learning Objectives	Essential Knowledge
LO 4.1.1 Develop an algorithm for implementation in a program.	EK 4.1.1A Sequencing, selection, and iteration are building blocks of algorithms.
LO 4.1.2 Express an algorithm in a language.	EK 4.1.2G Every algorithm can be constructed using only sequencing, selection, and iteration.

24. **Answer: C**. Option II is not true. A linear search like this will not necessarily yield a faster result.

Learning Objectives	Essential Knowledge
LO 4.2.1 Explain the difference between algorithms that run in a reasonable time and those that do not run in a reasonable time.	EK 4.2.1A Many problems can be solved in a reasonable time. EK 4.2.1B Reasonable time means that the number of steps the algorithm takes is less than or equal to a polynomial function (constant, linear, square, cube, etc.) of the size of the input.
LO 4.2.4 Evaluate algorithms analytically and empirically for efficiency, correctness, and clarity.	EK 4.2.4H Linear search can be used when searching for an item in any list; binary search can be used only when the list is sorted.

25. **Answer: C.** Problems involving maps have too many variables and unknowns to make the problem solvable with a "best" solution in a reasonable amount of time. Instead, we must rely on a reasonable or sufficient solution.

Learning Objectives	Essential Knowledge
LO 4.2.1 Explain the difference between algorithms that run in a reasonable time and those that do not run in a reasonable time.	EK 4.2.1C Some problems cannot be solved in a reasonable time, even for small input sizes. EK 4.2.1D Some problems can be solved but not in a reasonable time. In these cases, heuristic approaches may be helpful to find solutions in reasonable time.

26. **Answer: A, D.** Choice A is true because it does not guarantee the perfect solution. Choice D acknowledges the need for a quick solution.

Learning Objectives	Essential Knowledge
LO 4.2.2 Explain the difference between solvable and unsolvable problems in computer science.	EK 4.2.2B Heuristics may be helpful for finding an approximate solution more quickly when exact methods are too slow.

27. **Answer: D.** The team does not need to find the best solution; they need only find a quick solution.

Learning Objectives	Essential Knowledge
LO 4.1.1 Develop an algorithm for implementation in a program.	EK 4.1.1A Sequencing, selection, and iteration are building blocks of algorithms.
LO 4.2.2 Explain the difference between solvable and unsolvable problems in computer science.	EK 4.2.2C Some optimization problems such as "find the best" or "find the smallest" cannot be solved in a reasonable time but approximations to the optimal solution can.

28. **Answer: B.** A problem is said to be undecidable if no algorithm can be constructed that always leads to a correct yes-or-no answer.

Learning Objectives	Essential Knowledge
LO 4.2.3 Explain the existence of undecidable problems in computer science.	EK 4.2.3C An undecidable problem is one in which no algorithm can be constructed that always leads to a correct yes-or-no answer.

29. **Answer: B.** The programmer cannot guarantee with complete certainty that he has guarded against every possible means of attack. There is no algorithm that predicts how other people will approach a problem.

Learning Objectives	Essential Knowledge
LO 4.2.2 Explain the difference between solvable and unsolvable problems in computer science.	**EK 4.2.2D** Some problems cannot be solved using any algorithm.
LO 6.3.1 Identify existing cybersecurity concerns and potential options to address these issues with the Internet and the systems built on it.	**EK 6.3.1A** The trust model of the Internet involves trade-offs.

30. **Answers: A, D.** They can test the algorithm with multiple inputs to study its efficiency. Choice A uses observations to determine efficiency, and Choice D uses mathematics.

Learning Objectives	Essential Knowledge
LO 4.2.4 Evaluate algorithms analytically and empirically for efficiency, correctness, and clarity.	**EK 4.2.4A** Determining an algorithm's efficiency is done by reasoning formally or mathematically about the algorithm.
	EK 4.2.4B Empirical analysis of an algorithm is done by implementing the algorithm and running it on different inputs.

31. **Answer: C.** Empirical analysis relies on observation and experience to draw conclusions. Procedures I and II are based on observations.

Learning Objectives	Essential Knowledge
LO 4.2.4 Evaluate algorithms analytically and empirically for efficiency, correctness, and clarity.	**EK 4.2.4B** Empirical analysis of an algorithm is done by implementing the algorithm and running it on different inputs.

32. **Answer: B.** The computer should display "Banana" if and only if 'b' is pressed.

Learning Objectives	Essential Knowledge
LO 5.1.1 Develop a program for creative expression, to satisfy personal curiosity, or to create new knowledge.	**EK 5.1.1A** Programs are developed and used in a variety of ways by a wide range of people depending on the goals of the programmer.
	EK 5.1.1B Programs developed for creative expression, to satisfy personal curiosity, or to create new knowledge may have visual, audible, or tactile inputs and outputs.

33. **Answer: C.** The food "IF" is selected. There was previously no old cost (tax was 0%), and there is a new tax cost of six cents.

Learning Objectives	Essential Knowledge
LO 5.1.1 Develop a program for creative expression, to satisfy personal curiosity, or to create new knowledge.	**EK 5.1.1F** Advances in computing have generated and increased creativity in other fields.
LO 5.3.1 Use abstraction to manage complexity in programs.	**EK 5.3.1J** Integers and floating-point numbers are used in programs without requiring understanding of how they are implemented.

34. **Answer: C.** By placing the IF and ELSE conditions in the middle of the code, we can eliminate duplicate code, and also make it easier to reason through.

Learning Objectives	Essential Knowledge
LO 5.4.1 Evaluate the correctness of a program.	**EK 5.4.1A** Program style can affect the determination of program correctness. **EK 5.4.1B** Duplicated code can make it harder to reason about a program.

35. **Answers: A, C.** Using meaningful names and writing shorter blocks of code make reasoning about the code easier.

Learning Objectives	Essential Knowledge
LO 5.4.1 Evaluate the correctness of a program.	**EK 5.4.1B** Duplicated code can make it harder to reason about a program. **EK 5.4.1C** Meaningful names for variables and procedures help people better understand programs. **EK 5.4.1D** Longer code segments are harder to reason about than shorter code segments in a program. **EK 5.4.1I** Programmers justify and explain a program's correctness.

36. **Answer: A.** Examples of possible inputs and expected outputs will help the programmer write the appropriate code for various scenarios.

Learning Objectives	Essential Knowledge
LO 5.4.1 Evaluate the correctness of a program.	**EK 5.4.1F** Knowledge of what a program is supposed to do is required in order to find most program errors. **EK 5.4.1G** Examples of intended behavior on specific inputs help people understand what a program is supposed to do.

37. **Answers: A, D**. Good naming conventions and useful comments will not affect the running of the code, but will improve the readability.

Learning Objectives	Essential Knowledge
LO 5.1.1 Develop a program for creative expression, to satisfy personal curiosity, or to create new knowledge.	EK 5.1.1C Programs developed for creative expression, to satisfy personal curiosity, or to create new knowledge may be developed with different standards or methods than programs developed for widespread distribution.

38. **Answers: A, C**. Input testing and developing incrementally help develop a correct program.

Learning Objectives	Essential Knowledge
LO 5.1.2 Develop a correct program to solve problems.	EK 5.1.2A An iterative process of program development helps in developing a correct program to solve problems.

39. **Answer: B**. Combining correct and complete components will make a correct program. Working on a shared document can cause errors in another part of the code.

Learning Objectives	Essential Knowledge
LO 5.1.2 Develop a correct program to solve problems.	EK 5.1.2B Developing correct program components and then combining them helps in creating correct programs.

40. **Answer: A**. Code segment I iterates through each value. Code segment II uses the actual item value as an index, which is incorrect.

Learning Objectives	Essential Knowledge
LO 5.1.2 Develop a correct program to solve problems.	EK 5.1.2C Incrementally adding tested program segments to correct working programs helps create large correct programs.
LO 5.5.1 Employ appropriate mathematical and logical concepts in programming.	EK 5.5.1H Computational methods may use lists and collections to solve problems.
	EK 5.5.1J Basic operations on collections include adding elements, removing elements, iterating over all elements, and determining whether an element is in a collection.

41. **Answer: A**. The Digital Millennium Copyright Act does not require that documentation be published.

Learning Objectives	Essential Knowledge
LO 5.1.2 Develop a correct program to solve problems.	**EK 5.1.2D** Program documentation helps programmers develop and maintain correct programs to efficiently solve problems.
	EK 5.1.2E Documentation about program components, such as code segments and procedures, helps in developing and maintaining programs.
	EK 5.1.2F Documentation helps in developing and maintaining programs when working individually or in collaborative programming environments.
LO 7.3.1 Analyze the beneficial and harmful effects of computing.	**EK 7.3.1P** The Digital Millennium Copyright Act (DMCA) has been a benefit and a challenge in making copyrighted digital material widely available.

42. **Answer: D**. Asking the robot to move where an open location does not exist causes the program to terminate.

Learning Objectives	Essential Knowledge
LO 5.4.1 Evaluate the correctness of a program.	**EK 5.4.1E** Locating and correcting errors in a program is called debugging the program.
	EK 5.4.1K Correctness of a program depends on correctness of program components, including code segments and procedures.

43. **Answer: C**. The robot continues to move until the right is blocked. With every iteration of the loop, the robot first checks to see if it could move right. As it crosses the grid moving forward from left to right, the square to its right is always open. Once the robot gets to the other side, turns around, and moves once, the square to its right is blocked, so it does not enter the loop.

Learning Objectives	Essential Knowledge
LO 5.5.1 Employ appropriate mathematical and logical concepts in programming.	**EK 5.5.1E** Logical concepts and Boolean algebra are fundamental to programming.

44. **Answer: C**. Since the size of the grid is unknown, a repeat until condition is appropriate.

Learning Objectives	Essential Knowledge
LO 5.5.1 Employ appropriate mathematical and logical concepts in programming.	**EK 5.5.1E** Logical concepts and Boolean algebra are fundamental to programming.

45. **Answer: C.** After the repeat loop, the robot is facing south, turns around, and moves once.

Learning Objectives	Essential Knowledge
LO 5.5.1 Employ appropriate mathematical and logical concepts in programming.	**EK 5.5.1E** Logical concepts and Boolean algebra are fundamental to programming.

46. **Answers: C, D.** The tip and tax must first be calculated, then added to the meal total.

Learning Objectives	Essential Knowledge
LO 5.2.1 Explain how programs implement algorithms.	**EK 5.2.1B** Program instructions are executed sequentially.

47. **Answer: C.** APIs do not justify a program's correctness.

Learning Objectives	Essential Knowledge
LO 5.3.1 Use abstraction to manage complexity in programs.	**EK 5.3.1M** Application program interfaces (APIs) and libraries simplify complex programming tasks. **EK 5.3.1N** Documentation for an API/library is an important aspect of programming. **EK 5.3.1O** APIs connect software components, allowing them to communicate.

48. **Answer: A.** Only code segment III displays all the numbers. Segment I does not display 1, and segment III does not display 16.

Learning Objectives	Essential Knowledge
LO 5.5.1 Employ appropriate mathematical and logical concepts in programming.	**EK 5.5.1D** Mathematical expressions using arithmetic operators are part of most programming languages. **EK 5.5.1E** Logical concepts and Boolean algebra are fundamental to programming.

49. **Answer: B.** Only option III will add the final purchase of the month. The other options will cause the loop to terminate before the last value is included.

Learning Objectives	Essential Knowledge
LO 5.5.1 Employ appropriate mathematical and logical concepts in programming.	**EK 5.5.1E** Logical concepts and Boolean algebra are fundamental to programming.

50. **Answer: D.** In order to compare corresponding elements of each list, n must be able to iterate from 1 to LENGTH [list1]. Option I does not change the value of n, and Option II looks at the index rather than the value.

Learning Objectives	Essential Knowledge
LO 5.3.1 Use abstraction to manage complexity in programs.	EK 5.3.1K Lists and list operations, such as add, remove, and search, are common in many programs.

51. **Answer: D.** The URL has at least 6 separate parts. The highlighted parts are the protocol, top level domain, and the directory.

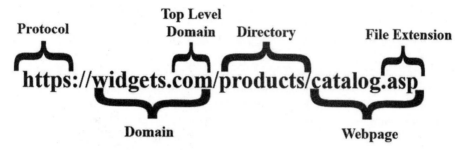

Learning Objectives	Essential Knowledge
LO 6.2.1 Explain characteristics of the Internet and the systems built on it.	EK 6.2.1B The domain name syntax is hierarchical.

52. **Answer: B.** Since each bit in an IP address can be 0 or 1 (only 2 options), each bit doubles the number of unique values. IPv4 is a 32 bit addressing system. Therefore, there can be 2^{32} *or 4,294,967,296* unique addresses in IPv4. IPv6, on the other hand, uses a 128 bit addressing system. Therefore, IPv6 can have 2^{128} *or about 340,000,000,000,000,000,000,000,000,000,000,000,000* unique addresses.

Learning Objectives	Essential Knowledge
LO 6.1.1 Explain the abstractions in the Internet and how the Internet functions.	EK 6.1.1F The Internet is built on evolving standards, including those for addresses and names.
	EK 6.1.1H The number of devices that could use an IP address has grown so fast that a new protocol (IPv6) has been established to handle routing of many more devices.

53. **Answer: B.** In order to be hierarchical, the IPv4 addresses are made of parts to assist sending packets to the right location. Consider the address 128.122.46.21. The 128.122 is the network prefix which identifies the network you are currently on. The 46.21 is the host identifier which identifies the machine on your network.

Learning Objectives	Essential Knowledge
LO 6.2.1 Explain characteristics of the Internet and the systems built on it.	**EK 6.2.1C** IP Addresses are hierarchical.

54. **Answer: C.** Public key encryption only works for the recipient. If Nate replies, his message will not be encrypted and there is no guarantee that Allison was the original sender.

Learning Objectives	Essential Knowledge
LO 6.3.1 Identify existing cybersecurity concerns and potential options to address these issues with the Internet and the systems built on it.	**EK 6.3.1L** Public key encryption, which is not symmetric, is an encryption method that is widely used because of the functionality it provides.

55. **Answer: C.** A couple of factors point to this as the most likely valid site. The https:// indicates that the site is secure and has a certificate of authority assigned to it. In addition, the order of the domain in the URL is indicative of a valid merchant site.

Learning Objectives	Essential Knowledge
LO 6.3.1 Identify existing cybersecurity concerns and potential options to address these issues with the Internet and the systems built on it.	**EK 6.3.1B** The DNS was not designed to be completely secure.

56. **Answers: A, C.** An exploit is a hacking method that takes advantage of a vulnerability in a system (such as a security loophole) and allows unintended access. Social engineering is a technique to psychologically manipulate a person to gain their trust and/or trick them into releasing confidential information.

Learning Objectives	Essential Knowledge
LO 6.3.1 Identify existing cybersecurity concerns and potential options to address these issues with the internet and the systems built on it.	**EK 6.3.1C** Implementing cybersecurity has software, hardware, and human components.

57. **Answer: A**. https:// is the protocol for how the data to and from the URL is transferred, and not a reflection of the hierarchy of the URL. In using the analogy of a tree, https:// would be the trunk that travels from the ground to the canopy where the branches (elements) then start radiating out and branching off.

Learning Objectives	Essential Knowledge
LO 6.2.2 Explain how the characteristics of the Internet influence the systems built on it.	EK 6.2.2B The redundancy of routing (i.e., more than one way to route data) between two points on the Internet increases the reliability of the Internet and helps it scale to more devices and more people.

58. **Answers: A, C**. It is important for young students to begin learning early on in their web surfing activities how to identify dangerous situations online. When they get older and the dangers become more sophisticated, they'll have developed an understanding of safe online behavior and how to avoid dangerous situations. Any communications with unknown people online and giving out real life information should never be done in MMORPGs designed for younger children. Choice D is incorrect because it does not allow for the possibility of questing with known friends who are also playing online.

Learning Objectives	Essential Knowledge
LO 6.3.1 Identify existing cybersecurity concerns and potential options to address these issues with the internet and the systems built on it.	EK 6.3.1D Cyberwarfare and cybercrime have widespread and potentially devastating effects.

59. **Answer: B**. Firewalls are designed to prevent incursions into your private network. Once a breach has occurred the firewall cannot search for, find, and remove any malicious software (virus, worm, etc.) that is already in your network.

Learning Objectives	Essential Knowledge
LO 6.3.1 Identify existing cybersecurity concerns and potential options to address these issues with the internet and the systems built on it.	EK 6.3.1G Antivirus software and firewalls can help prevent unauthorized access to private data.

60. **Answers: B, C**. Since .org is a top level domain, all domains that end in .org are considered subdomains of the top level .org domain. Likewise, any URL that contains widgets.org at the end is a subdomain of widgets.org. The URLs in option A are not subdomains but directories within the widgets.org subdomain. The URLs in option D are not valid URLs.

Learning Objectives	Essential Knowledge
LO 6.2.1 Explain characteristics of the Internet and the systems built on it.	EK 6.2.1B The domain name syntax is hierarchical.

61. **Answer: B**. Email accounts are very easy to set up and learn. New computer users can quickly get up and running and gain some knowledge before undertaking more complicated online tasks.

Learning Objectives	Essential Knowledge
LO 7.1.1 Explain how computing innovations affect communication, interaction and cognition.	EK 7.1.1A Email, SMS, and chat have fostered new ways to communicate and collaborate. EK 7.1.1C Social media continues to evolve and fosters new ways to communicate.

62. **Answer: B**. Extensive data from the U.S. government is freely available on a central website. Data from the Department of Education is available that indicates teacher shortages by state and teaching discipline.

Learning Objectives	Essential Knowledge
LO 7.1.1 Explain how computing innovations affect communication, interaction and cognition. LO 7.3.1 Analyze the beneficial and harmful effects of computing.	EK 7.1.1F Public data provides widespread access and enables solutions to identified problems. EK 7.3.1K People can have instant access to vast amounts of information online; accessing this information can enable the collection of both individual and aggregate data that can be used and collected.

63. **Answers: B, D**. A proxy server allows users to make indirect connections to network services. The proxy acts as the server requesting information so the filtering software doesn't know the school server is actually the requestor. This prevents any filtering from taking place. A mobile hotspot allows you to use your cell phone data plan to connect to the Internet, thereby bypassing the school's server altogether.

Learning Objectives	Essential Knowledge
LO 7.3.1 Analyze the beneficial and harmful effects of computing.	EK 7.3.1I Anonymity in online interactions can be enabled through the use of online anonymity software and proxy servers.

64. **Answer: C**. While the other options are viable alternatives, a real-time video conference with the research partner allows for a live discussion of the situation that can be recorded and reviewed later. The scientists can collaborate in real time as the situation unfolds.

Learning Objectives	Essential Knowledge
LO 7.1.1 Explain how computing innovations affect communication, interaction and cognition.	EK 7.1.1M The Internet and the Web have enhanced methods of and opportunities for communication and collaboration.

65. **Answer: A.** Of all the actions listed, only II and V are legal under U.S. copyright law.

Learning Objectives	Essential Knowledge
LO 7.3.1 Analyze the beneficial and harmful effects of computing.	**EK 7.3.1A** Innovations enabled by computing raise legal and ethical concerns.

66. **Answer: B.** While one could argue that all of the statements are true, the key is that the questions asks for positive impacts on society. It is widely believed that peer to peer networks promote more negative aspects then positive ones.

Learning Objectives	Essential Knowledge
LO 7.1.1 Explain how computing innovations affect communication, interaction, and cognition.	**EK 7.1.1N** The Internet and the Web have changed many areas, including e-commerce, health care, access to information and entertainment, and online learning.

67. **Answer: A.** A web cookie is a small piece of data sent from a website and stored on a computer through the web browser. When someone visit or re-visit sites, the browser can access the cookie to retrieve that data which may include information from previous visits to that same site.

Learning Objectives	Essential Knowledge
LO 7.3.1 Analyze the beneficial and harmful effects of computing.	**EK 7.3.1H** Aggregation of information, such as geolocation, cookies, and browsing history, raises privacy and security concerns.
	EK 7.3.1J Technology enables the collection, use, and exploitation of information about, by, and for individuals, groups, and institutions.

68. **Answer: A.** A cloud-based project management site allows for real-time, immediate feedback on multiple projects. By using a site such as this, the students can work on multiple projects through one site, give each other immediate feedback, and keep the most recent working versions of a project available.

Learning Objectives	Essential Knowledge
LO 7.1.1 Explain how computing innovations affect communication, interaction, and cognition.	**EK 7.1.1D** Cloud computing fosters new ways to communicate and collaborate.
	EK 7.1.1E Widespread access to information facilitates the identification of problems, development of solutions, and dissemination of results.

69. **Answer: A.** While sending a virus disguised as another type of file is very prevalent, it is not an example of steganography. In this scenario, the virus is not hidden inside of another file, it is simply disguised as another file type. Steganography, requires that one file type be embedded in another.

Learning Objectives	Essential Knowledge
LO 7.3.1 Analyze the beneficial and harmful effects of computing.	**EK 7.3.1G** Privacy and security concerns arise in the development and use of computational systems and artifacts.

70. **Answer: C.** Most GPS systems are actually accurate to within just a few feet. Many military and industrial GPS systems are even more accurate than that, due to the way they calculate coordinates.

Learning Objectives	Essential Knowledge
LO 7.1.1 Explain how computing innovations affect communication, interaction, and cognition.	**EK 7.1.1I** Global Positioning System (GPS) and related technologies have changed how humans travel, navigate, and find information related to geolocation.

71. **Answer: A.** Several major movie studios and music producers have filed and won lawsuits regarding the illegal sharing of digital music and movie files.

Learning Objectives	Essential Knowledge
LO 7.3.1 Analyze the beneficial and harmful effects of computing.	**EK 7.3.1C** Access to digital content via peer-to-peer networks raises legal and ethical concerns.
	EK 7.3.1N Widespread access to digitized information raises questions about intellectual property.
	EK 7.3.1P The Digital Millennium Copyright Act (DMCA) has been a benefit and a challenge in making copyrighted digital material widely available.

72. **Answer: B.** While open source software and free software are very closely related, there are distinct differences between the licensing that comes with each.

Learning Objectives	Essential Knowledge
LO 7.3.1 Analyze the beneficial and harmful effects of computing.	**EK 7.3.1Q** Open source and free software have practical, business, and ethical impacts on widespread access to programs, libraries, and code.

73. **Answer: C**. All of these applications would benefit a class of junior high students and are age appropriate for them, except for choice III, which is an app for personal productivity and record keeping.

Learning Objectives	Essential Knowledge
LO 7.1.1 Explain how computing innovations affect communication, interaction, and cognition.	**EK 7.1.1D** Cloud computing fosters new ways to communicate and collaborate. **EK 7.1.1M** The Internet and the Web have enhanced methods of and opportunities for communication and collaboration.

74. **Answers: A, C**. Motion detectors that control the lighting in a classroom ensure that school resources are not wasted. An RFID tracking system is computerized and there is no need for school personnel to access it unless there is an issue. These are the only two options that are fully automated. The other two options, while involving some automation, require school personnel to be involved in the entire process.

Learning Objectives	Essential Knowledge
LO 7.1.1 Explain how computing innovations affect communication, interaction, and cognition.	**EK 7.1.1J** Sensor networks facilitate new ways of interacting with the environment and with physical systems.

Appendix

AP® Computer Science Principles Exam Reference Sheet

ABOUT THE PROGRAMMING REFERENCE SHEET

This reference sheet provides programming instructions and explanations to help you understand the format and meaning of questions you will see on the exam. Each instruction is presented in both text-based and block-based programming format.

The programming instructions make use of four data types: numbers, Booleans, strings, and lists.

Programming questions related to any of these eight categories may appear on the exam:
■ Assignment, Display, and Input
■ Arithmetic Operators and Numeric Procedures
■ Relational and Boolean Operators
■ Selection
■ Iteration
■ List Operations
■ Procedures
■ Robot

Instruction	Explanation
Assignment, Display, and Input	
Text: a ← expression **Block:** a ← expression	Evaluates expression and assigns the result to the variable a.
Text: DISPLAY (expression) **Block:** DISPLAY expression	Displays the value of expression, followed by a space.
Text: INPUT () **Block:** INPUT	Accepts a value from the user and returns it.
Arithmetic Operators and Numeric Procedures	
Text and Block: a + b a – b a * b a / b	The arithmetic operators +, -, *, and / are used to perform arithmetic operations on a and b. For example, 3 / 2 evaluates to 1.5.
Text and Block: a MOD b	Evaluates to the remainder when a is divided by b. Assume that a and b are positive integers. For example, 17 MOD 5 evaluates to 2.
Text: RANDOM (a, b) **Block:** RANDOM a, b	Evaluates to a random integer from a to b, including a and b. For example, RANDOM (1, 3) could evaluate to 1, 2, or 3.

Instruction	Explanation
Relational and Boolean Operators	
Text and Block: a = b a ≠ b a > b a < b a ≥ b a ≤ b	The relational operators =, ≠, >, <, ≥, and ≤ are used to test the relationship between two variables, expressions, or values. For example, a = b evaluates to true if a and b are equal; otherwise, it evaluates to false.
Text: NOT condition **Block:** NOT (condition)	Evaluates to true if condition is false; otherwise evaluated to false.
Text: condition1 AND condition2 **Block:** (condition1) AND (condition2)	Evaluates to true if both condition1 and condition2 are true; otherwise evaluates to false.
Text: condition1 OR condition2 **Block:** (condition1) OR (condition2)	Evaluates to true if condition1 is true or if condition2 is true or if both condition1 and condition2 are true; otherwise evaluates to false.

Instruction	Explanation
Selection	

Text:
 	
``
IF (condition)
{
    <block of statements>
}
``
 	
Block:
 	
	The code in the `block of statements` is executed if the Boolean expression `condition` evaluates to `true`; no action is taken if `condition` evaluates to `false`.

Text:
 	
``
IF (condition)
{
    <first block of statements>
}
ELSE
{
    <second block of statements>
}
``
 	
Block:
 	
	The code in `first block of statements` is executed if the Boolean expression `condition` evaluates to `true`; otherwise the code in `second block of statements` is executed.

Instruction	Explanation
Iteration	

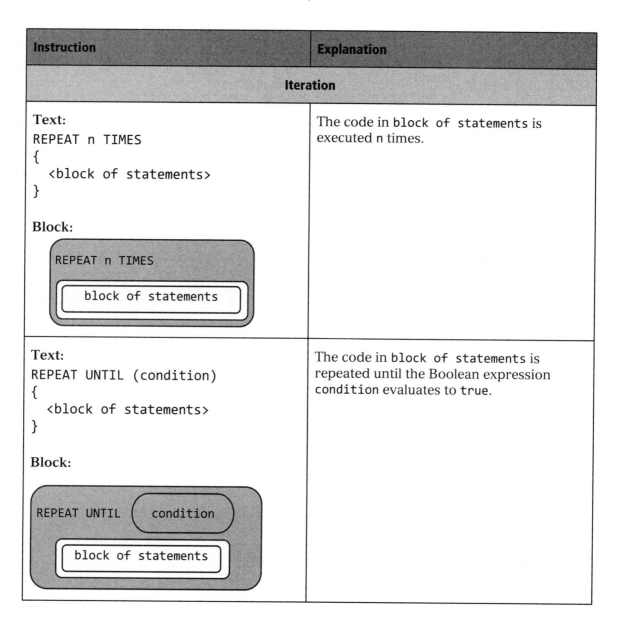

Text:
REPEAT n TIMES
{
  <block of statements>
}
 	
Block:
 	
REPEAT n TIMES
 	
block of statements
	The code in block of statements is executed n times.

Text:
REPEAT UNTIL (condition)
{
  <block of statements>
}
 	
Block:
 	
REPEAT UNTIL (condition)
 	
block of statements
	The code in block of statements is repeated until the Boolean expression condition evaluates to true.

Instruction	Explanation
List Operations	
For all list operations, if a list index is less than 1 or greater than the length of the list, an error message is produced and the program terminates.	

Text:
`list[i]`
 	
Block:
`list` `i`
	Refers to the element of `list` at index `i`. The first element of `list` is at index 1.

Text:
`list[i] ← list[j]`
 	
Block:
`list` `i` `←` `list` `j`
	Assigns the value of `list[j]` to `list[i]`.

Text:
`list ← [value1, value2, value3]`
 	
Block:
`list ←` `value1, value2, value3`
	Assigns `value1`, `value2`, and `value3` to `list[1]`, `list[2]`, and `list[3]`, respectively.

Text:
`FOR EACH item IN list`
`{`
`    <block of statements>`
`}`
 	
Block:
`FOR EACH item IN list`
`block of statements`
	The variable `item` is assigned the value of each element of `list` sequentially, in order from the first element to the last element. The code in `block of statements` is executed once for each assignment of `item`.

Instruction	Explanation
List Operations (continued)	
Text: INSERT (list, i, value) Block: `INSERT ┃ list, i, value`	Any values in list at indices greater than or equal to i are shifted to the right. The length of list is increased by 1, and value is places at index i in list.
Text: APPEND (list, value) Block: `APPEND ┃ list, value`	The length of list is increased by 1, and value is placed at the end of list.
Text: REMOVE (list, i) Block: `REMOVE ┃ list, i`	Removes the item at index i in list and shifts to the left any values at indices greater than i. The length of list is decreased by 1.
Text: LENGTH (list) Block: `LENGTH ┃ list`	Evaluates to the number of elements in list.

Instruction	Explanation
Procedures	

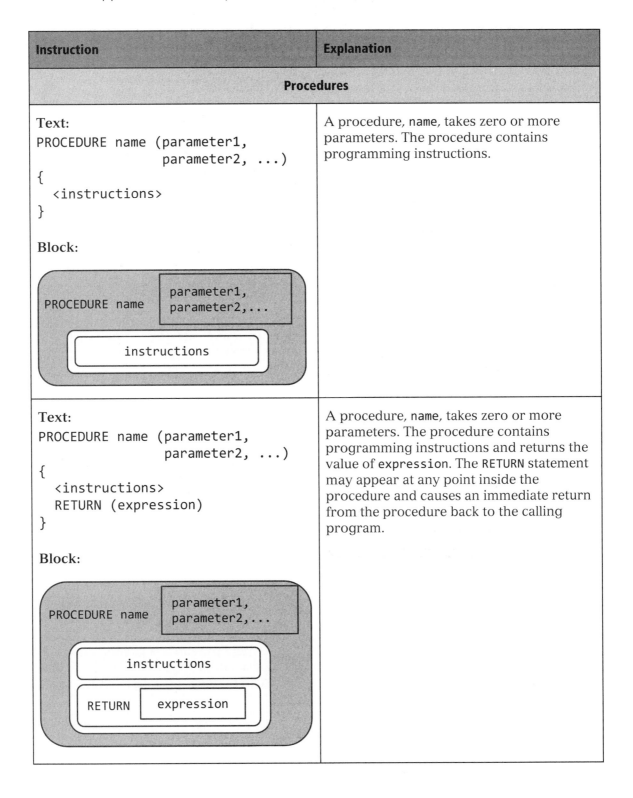

Instruction	Explanation

Text:
`PROCEDURE name (parameter1,`
`              parameter2, ...)`
`{`
`  <instructions>`
`}`
 	
Block:
	A procedure, `name`, takes zero or more parameters. The procedure contains programming instructions.

Text:
`PROCEDURE name (parameter1,`
`              parameter2, ...)`
`{`
`  <instructions>`
`  RETURN (expression)`
`}`
 	
Block:
	A procedure, `name`, takes zero or more parameters. The procedure contains programming instructions and returns the value of `expression`. The `RETURN` statement may appear at any point inside the procedure and causes an immediate return from the procedure back to the calling program.

Instruction	Explanation
Robot	
If the robot attempts to move to a square that is not open or is beyond the edge of the grid, the robot will stay in its current location and the program will terminate.	
Text: MOVE_FORWARD () **Block:** MOVE_FORWARD	The robot moves one square forward in the direction it is facing.
Text: ROTATE_LEFT () **Block:** ROTATE_LEFT	The robot rotates in place 90 degrees counterclockwise (i.e., makes an in-place left turn).
Text: ROTATE_RIGHT () **Block:** ROTATE_RIGHT	The robot rotates in place 90 degrees clockwise (i.e., makes an in-place right turn).
Text: CAN_MOVE (direction) **Block:** CAN_MOVE direction	Evaluates to true if there is an open square one square in the direction relative to where the robot is facing; otherwise evaluates to false. The value of direction can be left, right, forward, or backward.